A gift for

_____

Presented by

_____

The Best
Life Stories

The Best Life Stories

150 real-life tales of **resilience, joy, and hope**—all 150 words or less!

The Reader's Digest Association, Inc.
New York, NY / Montreal

A READER'S DIGEST BOOK

Copyright © 2013 The Reader's Digest Association, Inc.

Library of Congress Cataloging in Publication Data available upon request

ISBN 978-1-60652-564-7

We are committed to both the quality of our products and the service we provide to our customers.
We value your comments, so please feel free to contact us.

The Reader's Digest Association, Inc.
Adult Trade Publishing
44 South Broadway
White Plains, NY 10601

For more Reader's Digest products and information, visit our website:
www.rd.com (in the United States)
www.readersdigest.ca (in Canada)

Printed in the United States of America

1 3 5 7 9 10 8 6 4 2

Editors' Note

On our Facebook page in 2011, we asked you to tell us your life story in 150 words or less, and your response was overwhelming. Not only in numbers (though an incredible 6,652 of you wrote in), but in the plain grace of your stories and the bravery it took to write them. From this incredible outpouring, we selected twelve winners, who were published in the March 2012 edition of *Reader's Digest* magazine. They are reprinted here, along with another 138 of your dazzling entries (yes, that makes 150 in all!), because we couldn't stop at just twelve. Thanks to all 6,652 of you, whether or not you're in these particular pages. It's been a privilege to get invited into your lives.

The Best Life Stories

Barbara O'Dair, Executive Editor, *Reader's Digest*

One evening at home I pulled out a handful of your stories and took them to read in the car. Minutes later, I called my husband to come outside. Soon we were whipping through the stories (at 150 words each, you can do that). Page after page of triumphs, hardships, humor, summer days and war. Wise grandparents, broken promises, a drive down the highway with the top down. Long illnesses. New loves. Babies, lots of babies. Oh, and good dogs.

Amid chortling, tears, and nods of recognition was the revelation these pages bring: that each of us has our own life story that is precious and unique. That together these stories form a single narrative that says life is rich and complicated, rewarding and heartbreaking. That this is true for everyone. We're different, but we're the same.

I love this book. We hope you will, too. •

Let Him Go, Olivia

Alejandro Arbide, San Antonio, Texas

There I was. Upside down inside the swimming pool. Drowned. My parents were screaming. It must have been the summer of '63. It was a gloomy day. Every Sunday we went to my grandparents' house. My cousins and I were playing alongside the pool. I must have slipped. At three years old, I did not know how to swim. My mother was giving me CPR. More than twenty or twenty-five minutes had gone by. The ambulance had arrived. Everybody was staring at my mother. "Let him go, Olivia. It's over." Even my father had some feelings of resignation. Yet, she never gave up.

I write this story as a tribute to my mother, who, only four years later, passed away. And also in recognition of editors who made it possible for my mother to have read in *Reader's Digest* the miracle made by another woman utilizing then recently discovered CPR. •

Lazy Summers

Diane Archibald, Phoenix, Arizona

A single fly swooped around my head making that familiar buzzing sound. I started to swat it away, but then stopped when I realized it made me happy. How odd, I thought. A fly is bringing a smile to my face. I couldn't understand it until I heard the buzzing sound again. Then I knew. It was the sound of summer. It was that familiar buzzing that joined in the chorus of childhood laughter during so many lazy summers. Suddenly I had memories of straw hats and bike rides and lazy rivers; Fourth of July cookouts and campouts and hideouts; sunburns and secret forts and double-dog dares. The memories swirled around my head like that fly, reminding me of some of my happiest days. I decided the fly should stay with me today to accompany my thoughts while I reminisced some more. •

War Bride Runs for Congress

Flo Traywick, Lynchburg, Virginia

A college drop-out and war bride of World War II, I raised three successful children and had a groundbreaking career in politics with campaigns, White House visits, and Presidential appointments. At 62, I ran for Congress, the first woman in Virginia to be nominated by a major party. Served 16 years (4 terms) as one of Virginia's two elected representatives on the Republican National Committee, serving on the Executive Committee. On first-name basis with Republican presidents from Gerald Ford forward. Served 10 years on the White House Commission for Presidential Scholars. Lost a close race for the state legislature but became valued aide to the majority leader. Along the way, I graduated from college at age 54, the same day as my youngest child. I was widowed at 82 and now, at 87, I have started Flo's Bakery, LLC, to market mincemeat pie filling made from my great-grandmother's recipe. •

4

Sometimes Life's a Rodeo

Davalynn Spencer, Canon City, Colorado

It was enough that the cowboy I married was a rodeo clown and bullfighter, complete with makeup box and blond wig. It was enough that he wore baggy pants and football cleats to work darting around cross-bred brahmans and other snot-slinging bovine. But when one of those 2,000-pound critters ran the length of him, tore off his right ear and broke several ribs, someone had to make sure the filler acts went on as promised. That's when wearing the pants in the family took on a whole new meaning for me. Shoot a balloon out of another clown's hand? Sure. Find "gold" in the arena dirt with a toilet-seat Geiger counter? No problem. Match my husband's timing and mannerisms? Not so easy. Comedy is a lot harder than it looks. It pays to pay attention, because sometimes life's a rodeo—and you just might end up being the clown. •

Picture Perfect Moment

Vickey Malone Kennedy, Norman, Oklahoma

On a cool October afternoon, I dropped off my seventeen-year-old, Mayree, for volleyball practice. She jogged off toward the field, then suddenly turned back, ran to the car, and leaned in through the driver's side window. "See y'all in a few," she said, waving good-bye to her baby brother and sister. Standing outside the window, her ponytail swaying slowly in the breeze, bathed in the glow of the setting sun behind her, she looked like an angel encircled by a golden halo, like a Fra Angelico painting. I don't recall if I told her how much I loved her, or how proud I was of the amazing young woman she had become, before driving away that day. I never saw her alive again. But I thank God every day for leaving me with that beautiful final image of her. •

Loving Middle School

Guida Detamore, Boca Raton, Florida

People think I'm crazy for teaching middle-schoolers. The truth is that I enjoy learning about life from my students. Here's what they've taught me. You can be angry at someone one day and be best friends by the next if you're just willing to communicate. Asking for help can be scary but usually works. Snacks should always be shared; they taste better that way. You can start believing in yourself if you make time to study for a test and then pass it. Once in a while, you just need to put your head on your desk and rest. But most importantly, it's never a bad day to giggle and smile. •

Homeward Bound

Jim Ruland, San Diego, California

When I was in the navy, I drank like a sailor. When I got out of the navy, I drank like a sailor. You could say I went overboard. Swam with sharks and chased mermaids. Spent all my clams in the octopus's garden. The deeps and the darks suited me fine. Closing time came; I looked around. I was all alone in Davy Jones's lockup. Looked for a way out, but there was no ship in the bottle. Just more bottles, and every one an ocean. Took a long time before I settled on the bottom. But look! A boat on the horizon. A life raft with my wife and daughter in it. "You're here," they cheered. "Take us ashore!" "I'm just a drunken sailor," I said. My wife reeled me in. "No, you're the captain." I looked to the stars and plotted our course for home. •

First-Time Mom
at Age Sixty

Nan McNamara, Sun City Center, Florida

It was the seventies and Women's Lib said I could have it all. Marriage and motherhood could wait. After college, I worked; traveled; learned to fly, scuba dive, and white-water raft. I was forty-eight, however, when I finally married. Too late for that last "bucket list" wish, motherhood. Or so I thought.

My son Jeff arrived when I was sixty. My hubby Ken's son was thirty-eight, six feet tall, and unable to manage his own life anymore due to Huntington's disease. Jeff unknowingly received this incurable genetic neurological disease from his biological mother. From me, he would receive the benefits of a nursing education as well as a mother's love. This sweet, uncomplaining man-child is now in diapers, can't speak, and is spoon-fed. It's never too late to experience the joy and heartache of motherhood in whatever form it takes. Excuse me now. My baby needs me. •

Ninety-Day Wonder

Daniel Campion, APO, AP

My life pivots around a form letter I received in the mail in 1980. The letter was addressed to "Recent College Graduate" and held out the opportunity to attend the air force's Officer Training School. If I completed the training, I would receive my commission and become what was known as a Ninety-Day Wonder.

I don't know how they got my name and address, I don't know why I just didn't toss the letter, and I don't know why I followed through to become an officer. My family was astounded by my decision. Though I felt a sense of calling, it was easier for me to tell them I wanted to see the world. After more than thirty years, my mother still hasn't forgiven me for leaving home. But she still takes pleasure in reminding me about my first exotic assignment, to Rapid City, South Dakota. •

11

The Quality of Circles

Bruce May, Smyrna, Tennessee

Sitting on her mother's lap, reading *The Book of Shapes*, my daughter came to the triangle page. "What's this shape?" her mom asked. Wheels of cogitation began to spin (signified by a mouth scrunched to one side) and after a brief pause (and with the certainty of a jury foreman) she said, "A circle." Mom asked her, "Are you sure?" (As she did whenever an answer was incorrect.) But my daughter, sensing that something was amiss, said, "Yep," and then pausing, added, "but it's not a very good one." •

Do Angels Exist?

Steve Gaal, La Quinta, California

Yes—in folklore, fairy tales, and religious text, and on a lonely stretch of highway in Oklahoma. Driving my old station wagon on a seemingly endless highway in rural Oklahoma, my front hood popped open into a vertical position while I was doing fifty-five in the right lane. In a split second, darkness enveloped me. Shaken, I eased onto the right shoulder. In the middle of nowhere, with no tools, I gazed at the horizon. I saw cornfields, but not a soul in sight. Suddenly a man appeared out of seemingly thin air. Without uttering one word, he reached into the side pockets of his overalls and came up with an assortment of tools. With the dexterity of a mechanic, he fixed my broken hood latch. I raised my face to thank him profusely, but all I saw was empty space where he stood a few seconds ago. •

Morning

Betty Goldstein, Sherman Oaks, California

Daybreak. Cockatiel opens black eyes and unfolds gray wings. Repeats his name: Papagana Papagana. Papagana tosses kibbles. Prefers seeds. Muffin jumps on bed. He's not allowed on furniture. I put Muffin outside while husband sleeps. Muffin barks. Bring Muffin inside to avoid another complaint from neighbor— a man allergic to pets, children, and noise. Muffin eats kibbles under birdcage. Runs to teenager's room, hops on bed, and licks teenager's face. Teenager stretches. Textbooks, remote control, and cell phone drop to floor. In pajamas and bunny slippers, I step outside. Bring in waterlogged newspaper. Front lawn still wet from last night's rain. From out of nowhere are hundreds of snails—the same used in French restaurants—but I keep kosher. Accidentally crush escargot. Remove slipper. My rose garden, an explosion of colorful blooms, is framed within rainbow's arc. On one foot, I begin my morning prayers of gratitude. •

Christmas in a Vending Machine

James Jennings, New Hartford, Iowa

In 1997, I was in Vermont and was long-distance friends with a Mississippi girl. After visiting in early December, we were in love. On Christmas Eve, I found an airline running a last-minute special from Memphis to Boston. When it came time for Christmas dinner, I learned that everything in Boston was closed on Christmas night. We gathered our change and raided the hotel vending machine. Our Christmas dinner was Funyuns, Hot Fries, Fritos, Snickers, and Cokes while watching TV. It was perfect. Parting was heartbreaking but temporary. We were married by August. We look back on our "vending machine" Christmas and recognize how special it was.

Some people live their whole lives hoping for a special moment like that. Christmas is not about where you are. It's not about extravagant meals. It's all about who you are with, grasping that moment and appreciating how special it is. •

With Each Breath

Leah Chandra, Los Angeles, California

There was a first breath, and a smile, to find there is love. I was born to a religion of yoga, where breath is life. I became inspired to sing, where breath is song. I wrote words to challenge those things that don't seem right, where breath is thought. I then took to the stage, where breath is focus. I hear the words of others, where breath is knowledge. I have found passion in the touch of another, where breath is pleasure. I've felt pain and fear and have struggled, where breath is freedom. I have found freedom in friendship and solidarity, where breath is love. My life is made up of these breaths. •

An Old Soul

Amy Schaller, Tucson, Arizona

Born at home, delivered by Dad. First baby. "There's an old soul," the elders said. Raised with freedom and encouraged to be curious. A child of the great outdoors, both desert and pines. "Three going on thirty," Mom mumbled. Big sister to baby brother. Big spirit in a little body. Determined, stubborn, inquisitive, and strong. Always learning. Working-class girl goes to college, twice. But still paints houses with Dad and is handy with a brush. Never stops working. Seeks perfection, a great strength and flaw. Wants to travel, to write, to love and be loved. Most of all, wants to take care of loved ones. Now thirty-five and still learning the language of life. What next? Marriage? Children? Fame? Fortune? Many stones still unturned. Now Dad has cancer. Must be stronger than ever. The journey unfolds and the rest is yet to be written. •

Two Sets of Parents

Kimberly Harris, Palmetto, Georgia

I was born to a young soldier and his young wife. Two years later, I became the only daughter of a retired sergeant and his wife with three sons. At the age of twenty-two, after getting married and giving birth to my own daughter, I reunited with my birth parents, who were still married. They apologized for giving me away and asked for forgiveness. I advised them that everything happens for a reason and I had forgiven them long ago. Reader, my two sets of parents have taught me very different life lessons. My birth parents taught me to be resilient and flexible when life changes unexpectedly. My adoptive parents taught me to forgive when those changes are caused by others or even me. I feel blessed to have two sets of parents who have given me tools for survival. Thank you for letting me share my story with you. •

Life's Mysterious Buttons

Tamira Hartman, Raytown, Missouri

Mom passed in January. Slowly, I've been going through her things. I happened upon her button box. Not sure what it is about boxes of mismatched buttons that we hold so dear, but we do. Mom's was an old powder box, which was appropriate because she loved dusting powder. Interesting, the odd things I found in the box. A bartender's union pin, tweezers, an old penny, a lapel pin, a miniature Scottish terrier. Where did they come from? Why did she keep them? I imagined the stories. I touched each button and could see her placing it in the box for a "might need someday." This mysterious little box had the power to draw memories of her from deep within my heart. It is the most precious gift she could have left me. •

Chase the Day

Audrey Hagar, Los Angeles, California

I was my own worst fortune teller. The future just meant more disappointment. Childhood trauma was my excuse to stay closed and overly cautious. Why invite more shame and pain? Then I met Chase. The pound called her unadoptable. They said years of physical and mental abuse prevented her from being "normal." She would be better off dead. We took her home. Maybe I saw myself in this dog. At first she snarled and tried to bite us. I understood that need to put up a tough front. But then Chase became open, happy, and fearless. She didn't bear grudges against humans. She explored her new world and wrestled her new dog friends. She didn't dwell on the past as permission to avoid adventure. Chase, as usual, perches on my back as I type this story about a creature who now embraces the future without looking over her shoulder. •

My Funny Life

Barbara Nollman, Port Richey, Florida

Life has been all about learning lessons. First, don't fall in love at thirteen, but if you do, don't have four children by age twenty-three, because if you do, you will be very strict, and if you were, don't marry a man who isn't around to help, but if you do, make sure he doesn't work two jobs, but if he does, try not to be too lonely, but if you are, do not move to rural New York and run a resort/restaurant with four teenagers, but if you do, move back to the city and get a lesson in humility as a secretary, but if you do, make sure your knees don't wear out or you will have to retire to Florida like I did with the guy I fell in love with fifty-nine years ago, and if you did, well, it wasn't such a bad life after all. •

The Easy Path

Lauren Marino, Flint, Michigan

I went to Yale. I wanted to be a writer, but I majored in Comp Sci. I thought I'd never make it writing books, so I took the safe road. The easy path. Two years down that road the migraines started, followed by depression and anxiety. I became allergic to Computer Science; my body and mind rebelled against it. At the end of my senior year, I was driven to the emergency room of the local hospital. My head was spinning so badly, I couldn't stand up. I only ever found one doctor who could tell me what was wrong. "Computer Science isn't what you really want to do," he said. "This is your heart's way of telling you that." I left Yale, picked up a pen, and I started to write. It's hard. But the hardest thing I've ever done is try to take the easy path in life. •

You Just Never Know

Judy Paton, Cascade, Montana

After WWI, many of our soldiers returned home with war brides. My aunt Maggie's mother was one of them. She came from France and taught French lessons privately to area children. Sometimes my aunt Maggie (Madeline by birth) would play with one student while her mother was busy with the sibling. One morning John was free to play while his brother Joseph had his lesson. The game was hide and seek, and my aunt was "it." John found a splendid hiding place in a kitchen cupboard. My aunt, having home field advantage, realized where he was and shut the door, trapping him. There he stayed until Madeline's mother came looking for him and heard tapping and a little voice calling, "Madame? Madame?" Years later my aunt watched John Fitzgerald Kennedy take the oath of office. "Oh," she gasped. "I locked the president of the United States under the kitchen sink!" •

Night Blooming

Alicia Gifford, Burbank, California

Out my bedroom window to the thick, cool grass; the hot night air is spiked with jasmine. He sneaks out the back from his house next door (his parents drink and my mom sleeps the exhausted sleep of single mothers), pimply, shower-damp, brown-eyed, and sixteen, smelling of soap and nerves. We're clumsy, thrilled, ragged with yearning, first love eventually followed by first heartbreak. Flash-forward, astonishingly, forty-some years, a brave new world of cell phones, the Internet, and Facebook, and there's his daughter posting about her father, that he's a good man, a widower now for two years. She makes him chicken enchiladas and French toast. She misses her mom. Her friends LOL and "Like" her. I conjure him with grayed, thinned hair and laugh lines carved deep in sun-wrecked skin. I'm fourteen again, inhaling jasmine, the night-blooming kind. •

Sometimes It IS
the Destination

Hethyre Baez, Chandler, Arizona

Wanderlust has served me well. My mom says I was hopping the crib rail before I could walk. I learned awe at the Grand Canyon and independence when I moved to Missouri for college. I learned patience at Disneyland in the heat of August with my three overstimulated and oversugared children. I learned that the French aren't as rude as many Americans might suggest, and neither are New Yorkers. I felt truly blessed to listen to live jazz in the French Quarter just four months before Katrina. That an everyday experience for some, like seeing a blue morpho butterfly take flight or a capuchin monkey eating fruit in Costa Rica, can bring tears to my eyes and instantly transport me back to those precious wonder years when everything from a bottle cap in the dirt outside a Stuckey's to the St. Louis Arch on a stormy afternoon was truly miraculous. •

Your Officer

Jenny Christoforakis, Chicago, Illinois

They shoot at me with weapons and words, and I fire back with courage and compassion. It is my duty to turn chaos into composure, pandemonium into peace, not only with my muscle but with my mind. I experience life and death and cry tears of joy and pain all at the same time. The lessons of love and despair I have practiced since birth have prepared me for today. I end my shift with more scars than when I began, some on my body, some in my heart. There are comrades I have buried and many I have carried, ones who held my hand from the start. I am here for your comfort, to serve and protect you, to catch the burden of displaced evil and deflect harm. I bleed, I feel, I care, and I am real. I am your officer. Jenny Christoforakis, Chicago police officer. •

My Father's Daughter

Amy Goss, Daytona Beach, Florida

I learned toughness from my father. We were burying my little girl today, the first granddaughter in the family. Focusing on my father, I vowed to make it through this with dignity. I wanted to throw myself to the ground and curse the God who had allowed this to happen. Instead, I focused on my father, the man I had looked up to and tried to emulate all my life; the man who had faced every adversity and triumphed; the man who was determined to solve any crisis in an emotionless and dispassionate manner with courage and grace. As the priest concluded a lovely Latin melody, my moment to shine had arrived. My conduct had been impeccable, and surely my father's approval would be forthcoming. Turning from the tiny white casket that would forever be etched in my mind, I saw my father stumble. Sobbing, he fell into my arms. •

Nick's Military Milkshake

Loretta Chadwick, Mentor, Ohio

My son, Nick, joined the army reserves back in 2000. Come 2006, and he was sent to Iraq for one year. I prayed and had my church pray for his safety and trusted God for it. After his return, he shared the following story at a family gathering. He was leaving the dining facility one day and saw they were offering mango milkshakes. He had never heard of that flavor, so he decided at the last minute to stop and get one. Upon leaving the building, a bomb came over the wall and hit the ground in front of him, knocking him off his feet. He said his first thought was "D***, there goes my mango milkshake!" My first thought upon hearing about this was "Praise the Lord for life-saving mango milkshakes!" •

An Even Swap

C. A. Hamilton, Aurora, Illinois

When I got engaged in my early twenties, my wife-to-be was a soft-spoken young lady who rarely raised her voice or spouted off a retort, regardless of the often-snarky remarks I made about one thing or another. One day, I asked her why WE got engaged but SHE got a diamond ring. She said, "Well, you're getting me." I said, "But you're getting me!" "Right," she replied, just as calm as you please. "And you had to put up a diamond ring to make it an even swap." •

The Sweet Life

Lindsay Hunter, Los Angeles, California

There are things no one wants: slivers, cancer, road rage, breaking the last of the china. The time your grandmother goes in to have her leg amputated and an orderly steals her engagement ring. It's not that these things are good; they are, truly, awful. The moment of moments, however, is when everything you do want—waking up warm against your husband's chest, the right kind of attention in a crowded room, the incredible magic of your child—reveals itself as the story of your misfortunes told in mirror type. I am a bona fide crazy person. I have prescriptions, and practices; with their help I have, unexpectedly, gotten pretty good at life. And what I have now are precisely the blessings that a broken life turned out not to preclude, but, to my astonishment, to produce: actual love; safety; sweetness that threatens to never end. •

A Meaningless Diagnosis

Brian Mayer, Antelope, California

Most would not smile in my position. I sat across from the psychiatrist, holding my wife's hand as our two-year-old son played inattentively in the background. "The severity of your son's autism will likely prevent him from ever being independent. It is very possible that he will never speak or have friends. The comorbidity of mental retardation will compound these challenges." The psychiatrist paused and examined our expressions. My wife clenched my hand a little tighter, but she, too, smiled because we knew firsthand that the diagnosis was meaningless: At age three, a psychologist told my parents the same thing about me. •

My Life, Your Life?

Jennifer Stimpson, Jacksonville, North Carolina

It's a path: At first, you follow the one laid before you. Then you blaze anew. Then you realize some twists and turns got you quite far from where you intended to be until, after backtracking a few steps, you see that you were rushing and did not properly orienteer. When you deliriously step ahead, exhausted, and find yourself a clearing, you realize it is exactly where you need to be—but had not imagined the true and pure joy of arrival until this very moment. And the path you originally sought took you where you never thought you wanted to go. And where you were taught to go turned out to be a locale that you are content to never, ever visit. Because where you are instead is the best damn place you have ever, ever been. •

Crybaby

Joe Rhatigan, Asheville, North Carolina

The boys in my neighborhood called me crybaby. I avoided situations that could set me off: I stayed away from bullies, tried not to draw the attention of teachers. But inevitably, a bee sting, a cherished apple dropped in the dirt, would bring me to tears. I remember the day I ran to the garage to get a Wiffle ball bat. I turned my ankle on the hose stretched across the driveway and fell. I gasped. With slow-motion clarity, I saw my harsh choice: Be a crybaby or grow up. My best friend patted me on the back, but I shrugged it off. My dad didn't look embarrassed—for once. I limped with pride into the house to get some ice. And with practice, each day it became easier and easier, and the boys soon forgot that I used to cry. Thirty-five years later, I wish I could remember how. •

Memento

Marni Kleinfield-Hayes, New York, New York

It was a gorgeous day, so we went to Père Lachaise, a Parisian cemetery. We played hopscotch on the cobblestone paths 'til we found the grave of Oscar Wilde and left red lipstick kisses behind. Naturally, the ghost stories started. Then came the things we were most afraid of. The girls listed them on their fingers. Then came my turn, and I couldn't think of a single thing. I realized I used to be scared of everything, of bad things happening. But then they did happen and I got through them. I realized it was only the unknown that had been frightening. Whatever came next, I could face it. There in the cemetery, we were surrounded by death. But the sun was out, the tulips were blooming like mad, and we were girls in summer dresses with lipstick-smeared mouths. Life was still beautiful. There was nothing to be scared of. •

Linda's Shoes

Leslie Jones, Oshkosh, Wisconsin

The first few years that I attended Gresham Elementary School, it was predominantly white. In fourth grade, the teacher came before our class to tell us that a colored family had enrolled in our school. She said that we should treat them as we would want to be treated. I was delighted when Linda was seated in front of me, and we soon became friends. One morning during recess, we traded shoes for the rest of the day. Linda's shoes were much cuter than my old saddle shoes, and they fit me perfectly. Linda remained the only African American in our fourth-grade class, but by the time I reached eighth grade, our school had become predominantly African American. Now, I was the only white student in my class. And only then did I have some sense of what it was like to be in Linda's shoes. •

The Reunion

Brian Morris, Houston, Texas

In 1952, three fellow farm boys and I made a vow to return to our hometown in twenty years…at noon on July 4. We imagined big changes in town, so we decided to meet at the southwest corner of my parents' farm. In 1972, I took my family back home without telling them why. I hadn't mentioned the reunion to anyone over the intervening years. At noon on the Fourth of July, I stood in my parents' farmyard staring at that corner, half a mile away, thrilled that the Reunion was about to happen. Noon came and went, and no one appeared. I spent the rest of the day wrapped in melancholy but enraptured by a stream of great memories. I have often wondered, but until 2010 had never asked, if any of the others had thought about the Reunion. By 2010, only one was still living. •

Angry Mother

Karen Dahl, New York, New York

I work so hard to control the imprint on their innocent souls because I know that their bodies may be tiny, but their brains are sucking in every moment, every word, every gesture. I can't depend on anyone else to do this work for me. It's too important. I know (theoretically) I can't do it perfectly, not without help. So I go to therapy to exorcise my demons, my frustrations, my anxiety. Forty-five minutes is not enough. So I take breaks—dinner with a girlfriend, skipping bath time. I work, sometimes, as much for the break as for the need to excel, accomplish, engage. I tell myself that this work, mothering, is more important than all the things a career could provide. At least while they're small. All of this to prevent my own children from becoming what I know I already am: an angry mother. •

The New Year's Eve Lamppost

Ann Cardinal, Morrisville, Vermont

I'll never forget my mother's response when I asked if I could go with my friends to Times Square for New Year's Eve: "My mother told me not to go, and I went anyway. I'm telling you not to go, but you're going to go anyway. Just remember: Grab a lamppost." We found a spot in the crowd a block from the glowing ball. Right before midnight, I was picked up, the crowd dragging me along. Just when panic set in, I was carried past a lamppost. Reaching out and grabbing it, I stepped on the base and lifted myself above the crowd until I saw my chance for escape. I often think about my mother's advice and find myself seeking that lamppost whenever I feel unwillingly carried along. My lampposts have come in different forms throughout my life—family, friends—and I'm always grateful for the support they offer. •

Pork Chops and Pop-Tarts

Jannie Holland, Chicago, Illinois

The morning after my father stole me away from my mother in the middle of the night, I had leftover pork chops and strawberry Pop-Tarts for breakfast. It was all he had around, but it was oh so good. Mom's boyfriend had been molesting me, and I had been rescued. I was confused. I was happy to be with Daddy. I was sad to be without Momma. I was scared. I was a lot of things. But most of all, I was safe. Twenty-three years later, home from college for the summer, Mom's new boyfriend assaulted and tried to rape me. I fought back and escaped. Life has taught me to fight. And that includes fighting for a relationship with the woman who gave me life. Loving her, like living, is just like that breakfast I had so long ago…a strange medley of the salty and the sweet. •

These Parts of Me

Joe Dornich, Los Angeles, California

On August 31 I lost my arm to the shoulder on a nothing of a road outside of Tirkit. The explosion was terrible and amazing. Heat like God's sighing breath and a noise that moved through me, and in doing so created a cavern because sometimes I can still hear the echoes. Later, I asked the doctor about the remains of my arm. He just shook his head; that part of me was lost forever among the rocks and the rubble and the futility of it all. But I was smart. I left the best parts of me back home in Raleigh in the form of a wife and our new son who, though I have yet to meet, I love beyond all reason. I know that when I am reunited with these parts of me, my missing one will no longer matter and I will be healed. •

Lost

Jennifer Dykema, Denver, Colorado

It's a strange feeling, going through life day by day, simply drifting. My whole life I've been driven: to get the best grades in school, to go to college, to graduate, to start a career. Yet when life falls apart, when my career isn't what I had thought, my marriage falling apart a mere six months after the wedding, my husband unemployed, the bills stacking up, when my clothes are getting holes and I can't afford to replace them, my drive starts to falter. Nothing is as I expected, and I'm unsure of my purpose. Confused and depressed, I make my way to a family birthday party. My brothers start arguing about the philosophy of teleportation across the table at the top of their lungs, and I can't help but smile. Here, at least, I know who I am. For a moment, I am content to just be. •

I Have a Sister

Angela McGowan, Chattanooga, Tennessee

When I was six, as the younger sister of an autistic brother, I decided in a very childlike way that I would not be robbed of the "normal" sibling experience and therefore proclaimed to my mother, "I have a sister!" Her response? Crying. It turns out there actually was a sister who would have been exactly one year, one month, and ten days older than me had she not been stillborn. This rocked my previously death-free existence. I won't go into the years of survivor's guilt from being the "normal one," although to this day I still laugh when it comes up and I say, "Me? Normal? So much for that one, Mom."

When I was twelve, I met Marianne. My best friend and soul sister. I will never forget the moment she told me her birth date. Exactly one year, one month, and ten days before mine. •

Making End's Meat

Kit Vickery, Shawnee, Oklahoma

At the end of the month, it's tough to make end's meat. You don't have much money to spend until you get your next paycheck, but you've still got to eat, right? So you have to do some creative cooking with what meat you already have at month's end when planning your meals. I thought that was what the idiom "ends meet" was referencing. Imagine my chagrin when I found out it meant having enough income to meet your expenses. Of course, when I verbalized the expression, no one suspected I was thinking in terms of ground beef. How did I finally learn of my mistake? By seeing it printed in a book. What life lesson did I learn? Read something other than text messages and e-mails. Read a book, magazine, something professionally published. Heck, you never know what you might learn from reading a couple paragraphs in a newspaper. •

Can You Point Me to My Hometown?

Greg Grantham, Atlanta, Georgia

"From the DC area." It's what I say when someone asks, "Where are you from?" It gets you there without getting too specific. What I can't answer is "Where is your hometown?" Upper Marlboro, Maryland, where I was adopted, caught fireflies, played baseball, wrote little stories, and made slingshots and forts in the woods. Great Falls, Virginia, where we moved for better schools, returned from college, where my parents live, and where we still visit for the holidays. Richmond, where I met my wife, bought my first house, and brought home our first son. And what about Atlanta, where I'm watching my sons grow, coaching their games, carving out a career, and learning to love gardening, guitar, and fly-fishing. My wife says, "Why does it matter? Who cares?" Well, Facebook does. They just asked me to update my profile, and it got me thinking. •

The Death Race

William Kearney, Maplewood, New Jersey

Running alone in the Canadian Rockies and about halfway through an eighty-mile ultramarathon, I realized I was in over my head. I figured nothing could be worse than taking another step, so I stopped. At that moment I knew I had a very simple decision to make: I could keep my feet moving, or I could give up. I kept moving. Miles and mountain ranges passed beneath my feet, and twenty-two hours after I began, I finished the Canadian Death Race. A few months later, we celebrated my grandpa's 100th birthday. Hoping he might reveal some well-kept secret to longevity, I asked him, "Grandpa, how did you do it?" "What, this?" he replied, deftly spinning my aunt in time with the music. "It's simple; you just have to keep your feet moving!" •

Meeting My Father

Livia Pantuliano, Brooklyn, New York

My father passed away when I was a baby. I never had a chance to meet him or hear his words...until thirty-four years later, when my mom passed away. While going through her apartment and deciding what to keep, what to give away or discard, I would make an amazing find! I came across a stack of about eighty letters that my father had written to her during World War II, when he was stationed in Europe. I had never come across anything written by my father, so this was a precious gift. For the first time in my life, I had a sense of my father...who he was...what his thoughts were. Finally, I had a feeling of completion. His letters hold a special place in my heart and are among my most valuable possessions for they gave me my father. •

My Wealthy Life

Jim Moore, Chattanooga, Tennessee

At sixteen, my guitar and I found a captive audience at the local hospital. I went from room to room and, miraculously, patients responded with smiles and laughter. Doctors and nurses directed me to Billy, a little boy battling cancer. I sang to him every day for two weeks, then one day his big blue eyes closed forever as I held his hand. I was just a kid, but I realized that music had the power to change lives, and my career path was chosen for me. A few years ago, after performing my song "Dreams," I was signing autographs, and a frail little lady with tears rolling down her cheeks gave me a bear hug. She told me she had recently lost her husband of fifty years and, after hearing the song, realized she needed a new dream. For years I thought wealth had eluded me. I was wrong. •

The Choice to Love Unconditionally

Anissa Duwaik, Coeur d'Alene, Idaho

One thousand five hundred twenty-one days ago, my body screamed out like a freight train pushing its way up a thousand-foot cliff. "Congratulations, Mom. It's a boy!" Overjoyed, we introduced our son to his older brother. My boys! God, I loved saying that. Three hundred four days ago (or thereabouts), my son started getting angry. Really angry. Dismayed, I sought out advice from everyone. Why is he so angry? He's only three! My good friend said, "Well, ask him!" "Mom, why don't you believe me? I AM A GIRL!" Confusion, depression, anger, and embarrassment finally succumbed to research, understanding, courage, acceptance, and now pride. My son has transitioned. I choose to affirm her as my daughter. I choose to love her unconditionally! •

Dakota

Robyn Pasto, St. Petersburg, Florida

Dakota. Perhaps you've heard of him. He's our long-coat shepherd. His endearing spirit attracts folks from all walks of life wherever we are, an outdoor café, the park. "Stunning," "gorgeous," "puppy," "grand!"—words used to describe this beautiful, gentle giant. Tourists and locals alike ask to take his photo. He sits, smiles, and leaves a warm heart for the encounter. "Can I pet him?" Lots of pets. "Can I hug him?" Thin arms of the Goth-clad teen wrap snugly around his neck. Strangers laugh, cry, remember love gone by, sharing their stories of joy and grief when their beloved companion's time ended. Many lives sweetly touched. So many friends made because of him. Such an enriching impact on our human life. Once in a lifetime a thing of such beauty is placed in your hands. What you do with it is your gift to the world. •

Magical Moments

Carole Vakanas, Rio Rancho, New Mexico

Divorced with two small children, I somehow wound up in Las Vegas in the early seventies. It hadn't been my particular life's dream to wind up working in a casino or later as one of the town's first female craps dealers. But what a spot to meet so many different people from so many walks of life. I learned to treat normal people as celebrities and celebrities as normal people. It worked. My oddest moment was looking up one day to catch Stevie Wonder playing at a slot machine with the help of an aide while Ray Charles passed behind him with the help of his aide, and neither one of the musical giants had any idea the other was there. There were a lot of magical moments in Vegas. •

Life's Trials and Trails

Linda Gerding, Hamilton, Ohio

Life blessed me with two great friends in the last ten years. The first entered my life just as she had completed chemotherapy for breast cancer. Our shared love of horses paired us together as we spent many nights in my barn awaiting the birth of my mare's first foal. I like to think the unique experience helped Lois through some very difficult times. When Pat came along to ride my other horse, the three of us spent many happy and often hilarious hours riding the bridle trails in Ohio and Indiana. We celebrated each of Lois' milestones—five, then eight cancer-free years. Then the unthinkable happened. Pat was diagnosed with uterine cancer, and this time the prognosis was not so encouraging. Still we ride, and we laugh, and sometimes we cry as we hope for one more of life's miracles. •

Sorry, Mom…

Meghan Thompson, Ferndale, Washington

I should have 2.5 children, a mortgage, and a dog. At least that's what my mother says. Instead, I've chosen a month-to-month lease on a perfectly temporary apartment. My "mortgage payments" go much further than most; instead of a white picket fence, they pay for Dublin, Rome, Istanbul, and any other unfenced yard I may find. I entertain first dates with boys of all shapes and sizes, second dates for the men who survive the first—and third dates, they're few and far between. I've settled into a lifestyle of not settling. Of striving to live each day as though it's my last. To live for a week, a month, a year, a lifetime as a worldwide tourist, a pupil of the human condition, an observer of life, love, and loss. I'm not a complete failure, though; I do have a dog. •

Letters

Gabriela Revilla, Los Angeles, California

J names have defined me. The name of my first crush, the name of my first kiss, the name of my birth father, the name of my real father, the name of my little brother who made me realize I had a father, the name of my first husband, the name of my grade school, the name of my college. M names have broken my heart. My first love, first rejection, first big mistake I can never take back. D words made me grow quickly. F words have inspired me. C words have irritated, excited, and consumed me. L words have destroyed and rebuilt me. K, L, N, D, and C names have supported, taught, forgiven, and uplifted me. They continue to teach me things every day. An array of letters has saved my life, has made me laugh, has helped me grow, has let me be. •

A Lesson Learned

Ann Paden, Albuquerque, New Mexico

In 1990 I left a big-city job to relocate to New Mexico and bought a small house in a predominately Hispanic neighborhood. Taking a neighbor's advice, I hired Juan Lorenzo to clean out the fireplace and help with yard work. He suggested spreading the ashes over the lawn "to neutralize acidity in the soil" and set to work. Returning later accompanied by a visitor from Chicago, we found the yard white with ash. "Looks like Chernobyl out there, doesn't it?" Juan laughed, brushing ashes from his jacket. I turned to my friend and asked aloud, "How does he know about Chernobyl?" "The same way you do," she replied. Her words came as a rebuke, but the lesson was not forgotten: Prejudice is insidious and can emerge unrecognized. But there is more to this story. Some years later that bilingual "yardman" and I were married! We now live in his house. •

War Angel

Deanna Cisneros, Swansboro, North Carolina

Crossing the border into Baghdad, my husband's unit settled in for a rare operational pause. He realized the extreme lack of sleep, but the perimeter needed to be secured. Soon, he was back home in bed, feeling the most comfortable he had ever felt...so warm...not cold at all, peaceful. Suddenly, he felt our daughter tapping him. She was tapping, tapping and saying, "Daddy, wake up. Daddy, Daddy, wake up." He woke with a start, thinking that he would be seeing our daughter's sweet face looking down at him. Instead, he saw movement along the horizon! Needless to say, the sighting was verified to be enemy forces, and the platoon was alerted in time. The love and devotion for her father came through in such a strong, spiritual way I will never forget. God used her to help! A little girl! We are all truly connected by love! •

I Didn't Know We Were Poor

Deborah Rowe, Arlington Heights, Illinois

I was born in the hills of Tennessee. There were five of us in our family. We had no indoor plumbing or furnaces. We got our water from the well and heated it on a coal-burning stove in the kitchen. Mom used that same stove to cook on. Our home had two fireplaces. At night Mom would heat our beds with a bed warmer. We took our baths in the kitchen in a tin barrel. Mom made all our candy and cakes from scratch. Our food was grown in our garden or my dad killed it hunting. Mom made our clothes, each stitch with love. Our home was always warm, we were never dirty, and our bellies were always full. No one ever went hungry. We always had enough no matter how many sat down at our table. Funny, I never knew we were poor. •

Thirteen Things I'll Tell My Daughter (Someday)

Aimee Harris, Atlanta, Georgia

1. It's okay to date frogs; they'll help you recognize your prince. **2.** Confidence is the best accessory. **3.** Even if you have unlimited texts, call. **4.** Heartbreak doesn't last forever, but it sure can feel like it. **5.** Your life will not end because we don't buy a car when you turn sixteen. **6.** Work like a dog in your twenties. **7.** Know one good dirty joke and one good clean one and the right times to tell each. **8.** Read more than you watch TV. **9.** If you're ever in A LOT of trouble, ask me to tell you the Aunt Sarah story. This will only work once. **10.** Making mistakes is easy. Admitting them is difficult. **11.** Vulnerable doesn't equal weak. **12.** Go to college, even if it's just for the life experience (but we're only paying for the first four years). **13.** I love you unconditionally. •

A Foster Mom's Life

Keri Riley, Ninilchik, Alaska

I remember the smell of her hair when she snuggled close, trying to crawl back into the womb from which she did not come. I can feel her fragile arms wrapped around mine, her soft cheek on my chest as she held on for life. I mean I can feel her. I hear her beautiful broken voice soar with glee because she was simple and the most basic things brought her such peace. I feel her sweet breath against my face when she whispered in my ear that she loved me. Her desperate hands clutching my shoulders like it was a pivotal moment in time that we both needed to remember. And I do. I remember every moment of the two years she was with us. I remember the way my soul felt the day I had to give her back. And how it aches still. •

Jumped Feet First Into Bucket List

Karen Baum, Overland Park, Kansas

Young and brave, I created a bucket list. First up, skydiving. My instructor sported a jump-related broken leg that made me question the "affordable lessons" touted in his ad. I boarded the junkyard-worthy plane. I also landed with it. Twice. On my third attempt, I vowed to jump. Hesitating at the open door, I felt a shove from behind. The pilot pushed me! As I tumbled through the air, I cried, "Murderer!" Saving me, the tether line automatically opened my chute. My peaceful descent was abruptly disrupted by the hard impact of the ground. Failing to deflate, the chute dragged me through a freshly plowed field toward railroad tracks. An oncoming train whistled its warning. Inches from the tracks, the chute collapsed. My instructor drove up alongside the tangled mess, looked down at my dirt-covered face, and said, "You should have picked bowling." •

The Power of Perspective

Brandy Harris, Ocala, Florida

In 2008 I was diagnosed with Crohn's disease. It affects the digestive tract with painful and embarrassing symptoms…and there's no cure. I kept a positive attitude and made changes. After a remission period, the familiar symptoms returned. My well-being waned. I blamed myself, isolated, and reverted inward. I sacrificed my energy to the illness. I was hospitalized and my energy returned. Suddenly, I became terrified. I knew the "ups" as I knew the "downs." I was waiting for the other shoe to drop. Then, I read a book by someone with Crohn's. She described the disease as her "teacher." The concept thrilled me. I could handle a "Crohn's teacher." Now, even on tough days, I create. My "Crohn's teacher" helps me put my feelings into something tangible. My morning ache is now a poem; my evening nausea is now a sketch. Struggles and challenges can be your fuel. •

A Moment That Lasts a Lifetime

William Aiello, Howard Beach, New York

There's a moment that lasts a lifetime. September 11, 2001, in a few moments, all that we were and thought we were was gone. Growing up, parents and teachers taught us how good we had it in America. The world admired, feared, and envied us. With vast oceans on two sides and a strong military, we were safe from attack. That morning I worked at a post office about nine miles from Ground Zero. Within minutes of the attack, we saw the tragedy on the television in our lunchroom. Outside, the sound of police sirens wailing, ambulances speeding, and roads blocked. No longer were we safe or feared. We came to realize that we were a society spoiled by television, sports, laziness, apathy. Suddenly, issues of leniency, open borders, immigration, and security that had been ignored needed to be confronted. America would never be the same. •

White Confetti

Sarah Mendivel, Chicago, Illinois

I've never seen it snow, but I've been in love. In this moment, if I acted on how I feel, I'd bolt down to the street. "Taxi! Downtown!" We'd stop by the florist, buying everything: daisies, tulips, anything snow white. Stop by a music shop having band practice. "I'll pay you anything, come!" We'd buy white confetti, candles. We'd arrive outside her place, prepare. I'd cover the sidewalk, armfuls of flowers. It'd be dark now. She'd walk home from work, music playing. I'd stand in front of her. We'd stay silent. I'd outstretch my hand, take hers, surprising her. I'd pull her in close, having waited so long to touch her. Breathing her in, dancing, violins, stars. Suddenly, white confetti would fall from above us—the taxi driver. When she looked up, I'd tell her, because she couldn't be in Chicago to see winter's snow, I brought it to her. •

Still Laugh,
with Grapefruit

Kevin McCarthy, Boulder, Colorado

"He has a proud walk," **said a homeless man** with an eager grin.
Jasper does indeed. He prances, actually. Partly it's husky ath-
leticism. Partly it's Australian shepherd joy in work. Mostly it's
shameless grandstanding. Jasper T. Fetchmeister insists on carrying everything— the larger, the longer, the better. He carried
the newspaper home half a mile for many years. Unfortunately,
we lived in such isolation that few witnessed the performance.
Every day, our thespian would step into deserted intersections,
striking poses and listening for applause. A couple of years ago,
we moved to the city, and Jas achieved the fame for which he
was destined. Kids and old folks point gleefully at the chipper
dog with the extra-floppy ears carrying an umbrella or a note-
book or a grapefruit. From Jasper I have learned to do one thing
well. Reliably, proudly, and with love. The rewards will come. •

Letters from Camp

Ashley Bias, Orange Beach, Alabama

1985. Mom, what's happening? Send me a package. Yesterday was fun. It was Sunday. Tonight is senior college night. I have a boyfriend. His name is Todd. As you know, we have to write these. I'm having so much fun! Last night was movie night. Tell Patrick that I told everyone he knew "hi"! And everybody said he was so good-looking. I have the same problem. Everybody thinks I'm good-looking, too! Ha ha. Just kidding. I need a toothbrush and stamps. I got in trouble yesterday for talking too much. I never want to come home. Love ya, Ashley. True story: I haven't changed a bit. •

My First Love

Charlotte Counts, Covington, Tennessee

He was my first love. And the thing is, I never even knew it. Thinking back, I now realize that he and I never kissed. It was enough to just be together, with his arm around me, riding around in his cool black Mercury. He was so handsome with his chiseled good looks and black leather jacket with upturned collar accentuating his ducktailed blond hair. I close my eyes and the memories come flooding back. The teenagers dance to music from the Mercury's radio, music that has been buried inside me. They swim, smiling, unafraid and innocent, in the bone-chilling waters of an area strip mine. He hands her, more than fifty years ago, the unexpected Christmas gifts, a green and white wool scarf and aurora borealis necklace. Forever in my heart and mind, these are the memories of my first love. •

A New Nurse

Michelle Dedeo, Seattle, Washington

My first year working as a nurse, I picked up extra hours doing home visits for a hospice. My visits focused around helping patients manage the acute symptoms that were causing them distress as they struggled to live with a terminal illness. One particular visit I made was to "June," a kind lady needing an adjustment to her pain medication. I listened as she talked about her long life (ninety-five years) and the fears she had after receiving a cancer diagnosis weeks before. I sighed and looked her in the eyes without any idea of what to say. She could see my struggle and said, "It's okay, dear. I don't want sympathy. Aging is a gift given to very few, and I have cherished it." Ten years later, her words live in my heart. The gift of aging isn't always easy to see and appreciate, but I try every day. •

I've Got Dirt:
Memoirs of Your Housekeeper

Chely Roach, St. Louis, Missouri

As your housekeeper, I know infinitely more about you than you do me. I know what you read, what you eat, what hides under your bed. I know if you're OCD or if you cram your clutter into three poorly hidden clothesbaskets the day I come. I know if you attend church or believe you're a pagan goddess. I know your politics, your birth control, and that you take antidepressants. I know if your kids are kindhearted or if they're Eddie Haskell–type jerks by how they speak to me when you're not around. I know I am a safe avenue to vent about your husband's lack of intimacy, the neighbor's affair, your parents' favoritism of your sister. I know to you I am "just a housekeeper," but I don't mind. In you, I have received an honorary degree in sociology. In exchange, you receive my discretion. •

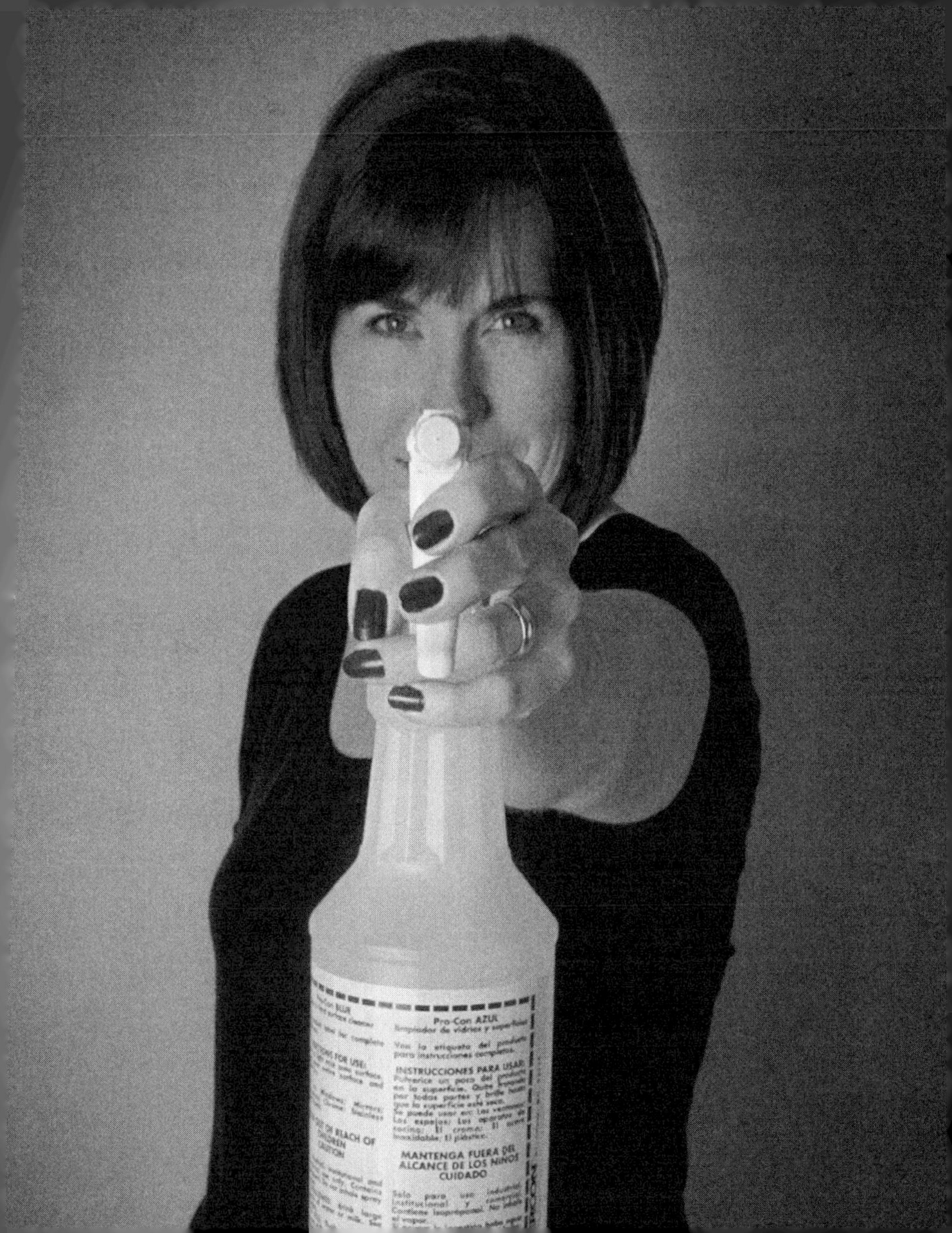
Pro-Con AZUL
INSTRUCCIONES PARA USAR:
MANTENGA FUERA DEL
ALCANCE DE LOS NIÑOS
CUIDADO

Ugh, the Job

Arthur Thomas, West New York, New Jersey

There's too much work! It's too stressful! We're not paid enough! My coworkers are complaining again. "Ay-yi-yi," I mutter, and close my door. The phone rings. It's the office downer. While listening politely, I take a mirror out of my drawer. Only 10:30 and I don't recognize myself. Thirty-three e-mails. Busy work. More calls. I slurp my third cup of coffee. It dribbles down my shirt and pools around the buttons. The office crier needs to talk. She sits across from me. I force a look of concern and shake my head until someone saves me. There's a knock. The office gossip: "Did you hear what just happened?" "No." I slam the door. A framed *Les Mis* Playbill cover falls to the floor. Later, I'm home, staring into the mirror, observing who I am. A smile forms. Quitting was easy, actually. •

Just Another Day

Jayne Shearer, Collingswood, New Jersey

Yesterday used to be my anniversary. Now it's just another day. It was a gradual erosion. Like a sand castle, a place was built with towers and bridges. It grew to something recognizable. Not Cinderella's castle, but a fortress nonetheless. Then the tide turned. At first, damage was done to the perimeter. Then each wave ate at the foundation until the crumbling began. Eventually, the big breaker came, overwhelming the last defenses. When the water receded, the castle was gone. No one would ever know what had been. It was created, it stood tall, it washed away. Now, I'm just a witness. I don't regret the effort spent while the sun was warm. I don't curse the forces of nature that swept it away. It's inevitable. Things change. People change. What remains…or what has been re-created…is the beauty of a pristine beach as far as the eye can see. •

A Daredevil Nun

Lula Mae Gostley, Evansville, Indiana

One day while performing the weekly chore of mowing my two acres of grass on my riding lawnmower, two nuns from a nearby monastery walked by and stopped to chat. One of them said, "I've always wanted to drive a tractor." To make her wish come true, I offered to let her drive mine. I set it at the lowest speed, and she drove off. I remarked to the other nun, "It's like driving a car." To which she replied, "She's never driven a car." Looking up, I saw she was headed straight for the fire hydrant. I ran after her yelling, "Turn it! Turn it!" I heard the other nun say, "She can't hear, either." •

Balloons in
the Morning

Gary Gaertner, Grand Junction, Colorado

Who decided balloons help sell cars? These past dozen years have taught me many things: answers for any objection; proper greetings for phone, Internet, or in person; how to make you buy NOW, parting with as much money as possible in the form of down payments, monthly payments, interest rates, and any and every product or service I can convince you is necessary and valuable. What a life! With crazy tent sales, slasher sales, and push/pull/drag sales, I've consumed more burgers, hotdogs, and popcorn than I ever dreamed I'd eat in a lifetime. Salesman of the Month, trips, contests, spiffs. They trick us to sell the cars the same way we trick you to buy them. I'm not a robber or a con artist; it just feels like it sometimes. I'm your friendly neighborhood car salesman. Sign here, and here and here and here. Thanks for your business. •

Baby

Lynda Ritter, York, Pennsylvania

As a child, when asked, "What do you want to be when you grow up?" my answer was always the same. "A mom." I had dolls, cats, and dogs that got my maternal blessings. When I reached my late teens, I was told my dreams would never be realized due to faulty hormones. I would sit in church each Sunday, praying that God would let me be a mother. Everywhere I turned, I was surrounded by pregnant women. I eventually got on with my life, did the college thing, the apartment thing, and then the married thing. My husband and I decided to try the infertility route, and after several years of trying, crying, and praying, I finally received my big wish. I was pregnant and thirty! Don't let anyone tell you God doesn't have a sense of humor! At forty-two, I had surprise baby number two. My life's complete! •

Dear Candace

Andrea McAllister, Cave City, Arizona

While watching my thirteen-year-old brother act silly as he plays with his friends, I laugh. Suddenly, I realize I have you to thank for that laugh. As a matter of fact, I have you to thank for every moment I have with him. Every ballgame he has, family trip we take, or joke he tells is a treasure. I know you have your own family now and you probably don't think about the time you pulled my then-toddler brother out of the path of an oncoming semi as we were on our way to pick him up from the babysitter (who clearly failed to watch him). But I think about it…a lot. Witnessing you risk your life to save my brother means more than you know. Especially now as he gives me a hug and tells me he loves me. Thank you… •

Hand-in-Hand

Misty Cline, Cromwell, Indiana

Many significant moments in my life have been marked by the holding of hands. My mother held my hand as she walked me into school on my first day of kindergarten. My soon-to-be husband held my hand as we walked across the Brooklyn Bridge. The tiny hand of each of my children curled around my index finger right after they were born. There was no moment more memorable, though, than the time I held the hand of my daughter and she couldn't return my caress. As she lay in the hospital bed, I held her hand all night, anxious for a response. Now, her little hand can hold mine again. We are determined to go hand-in-hand into the future, grateful for every moment. •

The Father/Son Hug Chain

Lara Dillman, Miami, Oklahoma

My ex-husband called uncharacteristically in tears. His father had never told him he was proud. This saddened me. From a close family, I feared this would trickle from one generation to the next unless I broke the pattern. I wanted more for my own son and decided I had to do something. I sat down to pen the "old man" a note. I wrote eight words. "Do not break the father/son hug chain." I was not brave enough to sign my name. Days later, I received a call asking if I had seen his father. Chokingly, he explained. His father had shown up and without a word reached out and held him to his chest. He was filled with emotion. Years later, after the death of his father, he informed me that among the personal effects they found one neatly folded slip of paper. It was not signed. •

The Ballad of Maren Kast

Tamara Christians, Haddonfield, New Jersey

She was there when I was born. She helped me make mayonnaise from scratch. She taught me to use chopsticks. She forced me to like squid. We drank bourbon and made plaster masks and discussed the world and all its trials and possibility. She is fly-fishing, kaftans, papier-mâché. She's the smell of a toasted English muffin with garlic simmered in butter, the sound of soft NPR jazz…so many things remind me of her. Over the years she coached me on being a good friend, a good Christian, a good daughter and wife; and despite the many times I have fallen short of my expectations, she never made me feel as though I fell short of hers. Grandma was an artist, a poet, a mother, a musician, a chef, a wife, a believer. She radiated goodness and warmth. Being with her felt like being home. •

Holy Water

Keith Hoerner, St. Peters, Missouri

During Mass, you knew when to genuflect and make the sign of the cross. But how to build a constant contact with God, a God consciousness that would guide your mired mental state to greener pastures, remained well beyond your understanding. For that, I feel sorry for you. I stand at the kitchen sink washing the one thing I took from home after you died: the Madonna and Child statue I meditated on, kneeling before you, being beaten, traumatized, loving you, year after year. I wash it gently, remembering the time you unknowingly soaked a statue of St. Joseph, carved out of salt, in a sink of warm water. You did not realize it would dissolve, desert you like your man-made religion. Only to return later, pushing your hands through the milky-white water, confused, almost frantic, as you thrashed about in search of what you had laid there. •

Miracle on Eleventh Street

Dorothy Rickert, Syracuse, New York

In 1936, I was ten years old and lived with my parents and two sisters on the top floor of a four-story walk-up on West Eleventh Street, New York City. For some obscure reason, our Christmas tree, now an unadorned skeleton, was still standing in the living room—in March. One day we sisters decided to drag it to the roof. As we laid it down, a burst of wind lifted it up and away it went. We ran to the edge of the roof and watched as it wafted east on Eleventh Street. An open city trash truck, half a block away, was heading west. The tree floated to the truck, paused, and dropped into the bed—a perfect landing. People on the street cheered. Henceforth, we referred to it as "the miracle on Eleventh Street." •

Running Away

Katherine Kingsley, East Smithfield, Pennsylvania

We all know the term *running away,* but in March 2011, I started actively using the term in a different way. When my son's father left me for another woman, I found myself left with our son, our bills, our life, and a lot of unresolved feelings. At the top was anger. As an outlet for my pent-up frustration at the unfairness of life, I began running. My sister purchased a buggy for my son's first birthday; and everywhere I ran, he went with me. As I ran through the anger, I found other emotions I didn't know how to deal with. Abandonment. Loss. PAIN. I ran off the emotions and sixty-two pounds. Life and the act of running seemed to simultaneously get easier, and now I run for my health and my enjoyment. I never thought I would say that running away gave me back my life. •

"EB"ing a Mommy

Courtney Roth, Ponchatoula, Louisiana

My name is Courtney Roth. The birth of my son, Tripp, changed my life. He was born with a rare genetic skin condition called epidermolysis bullosa. His skin is missing the anchors that hold it together, meaning any type of friction causes his skin to blister—inside and out. He was not supposed to live to be a year old and is now two years and counting. He lives in bandages and in pain, has a feeding tube, a breathing tube, and has lost his eyesight. Tripp has never spoken a word, yet he has touched countless lives around the world by his will to fight through this disease. My little boy is my hero and has taught me more in two years than I've learned my entire life. I know God has big things in store for him...whether it's here or in Heaven. •

Editor's Note: We are saddened to report that Courtney Roth's son Tripp passed away on January 14, 2012.

Twenty March Seven

Ashley Cohen, Boca Raton, Florida

Twenty March Seven is what I called my birthday for the first five years of my life. They said it was the cutest thing. I lost my front teeth and lisped the date correctly. March 27. My teeth grew in and I grew taller. I inhaled smoke and greeted my diary. They said I was still a kid. I hacked my high school bangs and thought twice about college. I waited for nothing and dreamt of everything. They said I would grow out of it. I pushed Mom's help away until my twenties longed for her insight. "I feel good," I said. My belly swelled and my wedding ring shrunk; it sits in my grown-up jewelry box. My two front teeth are as straight as arrows. My bangs are grown out. They say I will be a great mother. Her life story begins Twenty August Seven. •

Arctic Explorers

Michael Roberto, Danbury, Connecticut

Ah, the magical words were spoken over the radio. SNOW DAY! There was instant electricity in the air. I knew that as soon as I completed my shoveling obligations, I was free! As excited as I was, there was another family member who was even more excited than me. My beloved American Eskimo dog, Sitka, knew that a new adventure with her best friend was just an hour away. Once I finished my shoveling, I stepped through the front door. There Sitka sat at the top of the stairs with her tail wagging frantically. She knew exactly what came next. I strapped on her harness (which I knew made her feel like a REAL sled dog) and out the door we went. The neighborhood we both grew up in magically transformed into a wonderland of snow and ice. We were no longer boy and dog. We were Arctic explorers. •

Heather Montana

Heather Montana, Somerville, Massachusetts

My whole life, I thought I was going to be an opera singer. I trained, I practiced (probably not as much as I should have), I worked through terrible stage fright, and I spent many years of higher education on becoming the best opera singer I could possibly be. The whole time, I ignored the fact that singing didn't actually make me happy. I was miserable, carrying on with a profession everyone saw as romantic and artistic. Over time, I found an administrative job, which I've found I love. Who knew that doing paperwork and helping people in basic ways would be more personally satisfying to me than singing opera? I guess the truth is, I had to find an occupation I really loved and pursue it rather than live out other people's hopes and expectations. •

Christmas Card Humiliation

Deborah Teeter, Hesperia, California

After starting a new job I was given address labels by the department secretary. She said that the people in the department sent out Christmas cards. Christmas Eve arrived. I hadn't even bought Christmas cards. I remembered that throughout the year charities would send greeting cards for various occasions asking for donations. I knew I had a stack. I found them and quickly sorted them based on the pictures on the front. I selected anything that looked remotely like "Christmas," quickly signed them all, stuck on stamps, labels and threw them in the mailbox. I was proud of myself for averting disaster. A week later my boss asked me to his office and explained that he had had a terrible holiday; his wife had threatened to divorce him. I asked why. He said, "You sent me a 'Christmas' card that said, 'I think of you in my quietest moments.'" •

Good Morning

Kaitlin Jandereski, Bad Axe, Michigan

Sprinklers are swatting the sidewalk instead of the usual alarm clock bruising my ears today, and I decide to step outside. The air swirls through my nostrils. Enlivened, my lab greets me, tackling me to the ground and slopping on my face merely to remind me that she loves me more than anybody else ever will. The August heat hasn't clouted away the dew of the morning yet. I decide to go for an easy run. Or maybe I'll go for a hard run. It's whatever because it's my morning. A few roosters crow from the side of the Richards's barn down my dirt road. And I run an extra mile just to see them peck at each other. That "accomplished feeling" is tattooed to my chest all day long like a runner's race tag. By 7:00 a.m., I have already poured myself a glass of lemonade to celebrate life. •

My Tattooed Arms

Brian Falk, Ann Arbor, Michigan

People think they can judge a book by its cover. I wear my pain on my arms, but my battle scars prove my individuality. I was born crippled, fitted for casts on my newly broken legs as a newborn. I wore those funny-looking high-topped shoes when most everyone else wore shoes they actually liked, at least more than I liked my orthopedics. I fell from a tree when I was fifteen and suffered a closed head injury, changing the direction of my life. Because of paralysis on my left side, I dragged my leg. I couldn't play basketball like before. I had to learn everything over again. My personality changed significantly. I wasn't angry all the time. The bully disappeared. Basketball was my rehab. Thirty-two years later, no one can tell I was crippled or paralyzed, but they do stare at my tattooed arms, turning from my smile. •

Love Letters

Chelsee Pengal, New York, New York

In fifth grade, Brett liked me. I knew because he teased me relentlessly. One day, he stole the hat from my head and used it in a game of catch with his friends. Later, I received a note that said, "Sorry I took your hat. I like you. Do you like me? — Brett." My ten-year-old brain couldn't process the strange feelings I had, so I did what any girl who might like a boy would do when faced with this dilemma. I wrote back, "No." After Brett read the note, he immediately ran off and started joking with his friends as if nothing had happened, but the teasing stopped. Permanently. Almost twenty years later, I'm sure his heart has mended, but mine never has. It's a little-known fact I learned that day in fifth grade: When you break someone's heart, a part of yours goes missing, too. •

I'm Like You

Valerie Zane, Malvern, Iowa

I'm like you. I wake up each day and find the courage to live. I love to laugh, love, dance, and sing. I strive to do and be my best, to help others, to be healthy, to be alive. I have goals. Some I've accomplished and others, well, I'm trying. Sometimes I fail, but I keep trying because I know it's worth it. I'm worth it. My daughter is worth it. My life is worth living. I want to be happy. I want you to be happy. Like you, I have days when I need to push through the pain, pull myself up, face my fears, and forgive myself for not trying hard enough yesterday. I promise to try harder today. Like you, I dream big dreams and I hope, wish, and pray that those dreams come true. I believe anything is possible. I really do. And I'm like you. •

Can You Love One Child More Than Another?

Katherine Doe Johnson, Watertown, New York

As a mother of three grown and wonderful children, I am spending a lot of time looking back over my life. I wondered one day if it was possible for a parent to love one of her children more than another? I decided that it is indeed possible, and so I let each one of my children in on my secret. To my oldest child, Lisa, I told her, "I love you the very best because you were my very firstborn child and my only daughter." To my oldest son, Rick, I said, "I love you the very best because you were my first-born male child and the bearer of your late father's name." To my youngest son, Mike, I said, "I love you the very best because you are my baby." •

Some Moms
Shop, We Rock

Deanne Brown, Laguna Niguel, California

**Four years ago, six crazy forty-something suburban house-
wives** went out on a limb, bucked convention, and started a rock
'n' roll band. There was one glitch. Not one of us could play an in-
strument. But that did not stop us. We bought guitars, replaced
the couch and coffee table with drums and amps, and left the
dishes in the sink, stealing a few precious moments away from
our kids, husbands, "should and ought to's" to follow our souls
and play some rock 'n' roll. We practiced until we had blisters on
top of blisters and that up, down, up pattern was ingrained in
our brains. When I was diagnosed with breast cancer, we practiced in between chemo treatments. Last night we performed in
front of three hundred people at "Cocktails 4 the Cure" in honor
of Breast Cancer Awareness Month and six women who refused
to let anything stop them! •

Snake Bite

Erik Zeidler, Bronx, New York

The venom worked fast. I felt my body giving up. Still conscious for the moment, I felt betrayed. Snakebites are supposed to take hours to kill you, but only minutes passed until my heart stopped. The next two days were condensed into a few moments of vague recollection. From a distant chamber of my mind, I heard the echo of my savior's voice calling, "Kids from the Bronx don't die in the woods in Kansas!" I could faintly hear the rhythmic beats of the chopper blades, beating as faintly as my heart, which had been suddenly shocked back to life. I awoke to the warm touch of my mother's hand, appropriately present on the day of my rebirth. I was blind from hypoxia, but I could see my future clearly. I cannot deny my passion. Though they nearly killed me, I have dedicated my life to the study of snakes. •

Dressing Down

Iman Mazioum, Houston, Texas

I wear the Islamic headdress, hijab, while being modestly covered, and I am in my school's theater productions. Naturally, I participate in dressing room shenanigans with enthusiasm because only females are present. The first time changing into costume, I shed my loose clothing and heard a girl remark, "Wow, you have curves!" I blushed at the compliment. I thought to say something nice in return, only to look around the room and find every other girl wearing adorable bras and fancy undies. I looked down at my standard my-mom-buys-my-underwear underwear. Determined to step out of my cave, I bought seven sexy undies the next day. Slowly changing in the dressing room, I heard, "OMGEEE, LEOPARD PRINT! Well, I never suspected!" Suddenly I felt great, like I was the newest member of an unspoken club; it was my rite of passage into femininity. •

The Older Sister Era

Sabina Vajraca, New York, New York

Memories of my childhood are fragmented at best. They come in snippets, a sudden sound transporting me into the mind of a six-year-old Bosnian girl, while a melancholy smile haunts my grown-up American lips. But the moment my little brother was born is etched in there forever. Perhaps because it marked the end of my reign. My dethroning, an unceremonious affair, happened almost overnight; and I, as every monarch before me, harbored deep resentment and secret plans of regaining the crown. We fought, laughed, cried, and loved our way through war, exile, emigration, and New York City; but when one August, some twenty-four years later, he went to sleep, never to wake up again, I found my dreams of queenship strangely gone. Search as I might, all I'm left with is his laugh, contagious and disarming, transporting me to the older sister era instantly. And I smile, tearfully. •

Faking It

Kristin Goethals, Kingsley, Michigan

I'm great at faking it. . . faking the high energy, the constant drive, the need to be right, the feeling of accomplishment, being a great mom, a good wife, and an exceptional teacher. I love my kids, my husband, and my work every day, not necessarily in that order. When asked how I do it, I smile and have no words of wisdom except for this. I fake it every day. You see the four well-behaved little boys who bask in my attention, the meals I prepare, the perfectly ordered house, the highly structured classroom, but you've missed my real life. My real life is tantrums in the aisle, running out of diapers, arguing over the dog, lesson plans forgotten, headaches from stress, ulcers gnawing at my stomach. You miss the real me, where somewhere along the line it isn't faking anymore. My life is what you see and so much more. •

Second Chances

Josh Kilen, Port Orchard, Washington

I left her when she was six and a half months pregnant with our son... On Valentine's Day. Did I mention that's also the day before her birthday? Yes, I was a word you can't print in *Reader's Digest.* The next eight years taught me some hard lessons as I lived the consequences of my choices. One day, sitting in a Los Angeles jail cell, I realized that leaving her was the single biggest mistake of my life. I vowed to do whatever it took to win her love again. I went back, humbled myself, begged forgiveness, and did my best to show her the man I'd finally become. Eight and a half years after walking away, I was down on one knee, heart pounding, asking that same woman to spend the rest of her life by my side and hoping for the impossible. I'm so thankful Megan said yes. •

Silence

Michele Weisman, Brentwood, California

Silence, how I miss you. You were a great companion in this busy world. You provided nourishment—my own private retreat—the ability to think through problems to a solution. You made a "to-do list: tangible. Where have you gone? You have deserted me. You have run so far from my life that my heart aches to feel your presence again. I wonder sometimes if you were ever in my life or if it was only my imagination. I have come to realize that you cannot be around my children. They are loud. They scream, they yell, they slap, bite, giggle and sing! You cannot exist anywhere around them. I am sorry to see that you have gone. I hope to be with you again someday. Although it was an easy decision for you to leave, please know I am still adjusting to enduring without you. •

Snap Judgment

Dennis Jarden, Quincy, Illinois

A trip to the bank left me with a huge dose of humility and a change of attitude that has altered my life. Living in an area with few minorities, I was always alert to strangers that didn't belong in our community. As I left the bank, there was one of "them" in my vehicle. Approaching my car rapidly with a shout to confront the "thief" who was exiting my car carrying only a puzzled look and a smile on his face, his first words caused me to pause. "I'm so sorry. I thought this one was mine," he said, pointing to his car, parked next to mine, which was the same type and color. All my bigotry, deep-seated and ugly, struck me like a lightning bolt and left me, hopefully forever. I uttered a feeble "That's okay" as I recognized a great person, legend, and entertainer…Mr. Chuck Berry. •

Don't Ever Think You Didn't Do Enough

Laura Guillot, Jefferson, Louisiana

Meghan was an infant with a heart defect that I cared for in the neonatal intensive care unit (NICU). The day of her surgery arrived. As the hours ticked on through the day and into the evening, we knew the news would not be good. She was sent back to the NICU with multiple infusions and a pacemaker, only to be pronounced dead a few hours later. At her funeral, her father called me to come into the family room. He hugged me and said the words that have warmed me for years: "Don't ever think you didn't do enough." Here was a family about to bury their infant and they were thanking me. The little things I did for them—like timing her bath and feedings so that they could participate—gave them memories that they will have forever. After many years, I still carry those same memories. •

Worst Enemy

Greg Rohloff, Amarillo, Texas

Looking across the crowd at my fortieth high-school reunion, I spotted walking my way one of the persons I really had not looked forward to seeing. He had been a tormenter, a teaser, a prankster who had made me feel miserable. He grinned, called out my name, and started talking about himself and asking questions of me as warmly as the exchanges with long-lost best friends. That's when I realized he really hadn't been among my worst enemies, for the teasing and taunting had prepared me for the rough patches in life that always arise. Without him, I would not have been as prepared for adversity. He was really among my best friends. I can't wait to see him again. •

A Good Life

Julie de Lagarde, Los Angeles, California

My life began in her arms. Now I watch her holding my baby with great joy. I always thought I would be better than she at this. Now I watch, amazed, and aspire to be as good. I have had many opportunities. I have succeeded and failed. I have loved with difficulty and ease. I have achieved things and have sought meaning in them. I have watched from the streets of New York as our towers fell. I have searched for love and found it. I have found a job that I love to do. I have given birth in water at home, held by my husband; her life began in our arms. I have come to know what is important to me. I have found deep gratitude for my parents. I have found that for many, life boils down to family. And with gratitude, I have one. •

The Twenty-Fourth of July

Linda Sumsion, Bountiful, Utah

July 24 was Mother's favorite day. She joyfully fed generations of parade-goers who came to the park on that annual Blackhawk celebration. We five siblings testify to the popularity of her contribution; we peddled roasters full of Sloppy Joes. Her culinary charity defined our lives. Cornstarch pudding was a preschool panacea. Teenage fears were swallowed with vegetable stew. Peach cake accompanied birthdays and weddings. Churned ice cream salved the sting of fifteen divorces. Long after roaster and childhood house were empty, we siblings huddled in Mom's hospice room, hating the cancer that robbed her ability to eat, but remembering foods that connected us to her. Baked rice for Frank's furlough. Beet greens with tears at Sarah's suicide. Apple buckle for Dad's burial. Reciting our lives in recipes until that final day when she wondered, "Is it summer?" Her generous heart had guessed… It was the twenty-fourth of July. •

Invisible

Mary DeKok Blowers, Holland, Michigan

Lying on the rough logs making up the floor of the tree house, I took a slow, deep breath. I was looking up at cotton candy clouds and trying to spot the moment the dog became a dragon and the airplane an overstuffed chair. The shapes changed mysteriously when I looked away. Sometimes I felt I didn't fit in with the other kids at camp. Games didn't seem like fun—I was clumsy and had a hard time playing softball, kickball, dodge ball. I would even sneak to the back of the line if I could get away with it so I wouldn't have to take my turn at bat. But when I needed to get away by myself, I loved this tree house. It was magical. Somehow I felt like I blended in with my surroundings and was one with the earth. In the tree house, I was invisible. •

Lost Life, Gave Life

Casie Kelly, Spring Valley, California

I wanted to be famous. I never knew my father, and my mother, even at twenty-seven, was just a child herself. My childhood came and went very fast. I was surrounded by partying, drugs, and alcohol and subject to abuse by my mom's many boyfriends. I ran away at sixteen, addicted to crystal meth. I met the man who would be my husband and got pregnant at seventeen, giving up my addiction because I wanted my child to have a better life. We married on my eighteenth birthday, and had our third child at twenty-two. I am now twenty-four and still working on my degree. We struggle financially, but we do have love, we do give strength, and we do have each other. My kids know the importance of school and have an involved mom who advocates for them. I'm not famous, but my kids love me anyway. •

Evolving Farmer

Julia Boyce, Foster, Rhode Island

I didn't decide to become a farmer, it sort of just happened. When my husband brought home Cowie, a young steer, I made it clear that I wasn't sure I could eat an animal that we raised, let alone had a name. We never did eat Cowie, but he was the start of our transition to farmers. We began raising meats for ourselves. The "local all-natural" market wasn't big back then, but friends were begging to buy meats from us. We soon built our own butcher shop. We now raise all-natural beef, lamb, and poultry. We also process meats for other local farmers. When people ask me how I can eat something that was once in my backyard, the answer is easy. I want to know what's in my family's food and that the animal had a nice life. We don't name them anymore, though. •

The Secret Life of Dog Catchers

Shirley Zindler, Sebastopol, California

My blond ponytail swings, and my rescued Great Dane waits by my side as I load my rifle and shotgun into my truck. I'm an animal control officer, and I never know what the day will bring. I've rescued injured puppies, sick bobcats, baby ducks, and just about every other creature you can imagine. I've removed animals from terrible situations and pressed charges against neglectful owners. I've chased horses down the highway at midnight, assisted on police raids, and removed pythons from apartments. I've been threatened by gang members, bitten by dogs, and slashed in a cockfighting bust. I've helped animals and people in mudslides, floods, and fires. I drag home the abandoned, broken, and orphaned; and my husband and children help me rehabilitate them. It's a life of tragedies and triumphs, of tears of pain and tears of joy. This is my life. •

Later

Katy Sulfridge, Boone, North Carolina

I've always meant to be the kind of person who lives as if tomorrow might never come. Unfortunately, I haven't gotten around to it. Why do today what you can put off 'til tomorrow? Or the weekend? I am terrible about returning phone calls or e-mails, thinking that there is going to be plenty of time to do so. I'll be able to send that message tomorrow, when I can think clearly. I'll return that call next week, when I have more time. I'll stop by and visit the next time I'm in town—there's too much to squeeze in this time. But now I don't get that chance. It's too late to give you a call. You won't be there now when I visit. You won't receive an e-mail or a letter that I write. But I did show up to see you—at the funeral. •

Not Until It's Time

Shereen Hart Greene, Mesa, Arizona

My grandfather didn't like me very much, or at least he never bothered to show it. I was always hesitant to ask him anything because I knew I'd never get an answer. Sometime toward the end of his life at the age of ninety-eight, I became curious as to what he learned on his journey here, if anything at all. I formed my question to provoke an answer from him whether he wanted to give it or not. "Poppy," I asked, "did you ever get it all figured out?" He didn't blink or ask me to explain what I meant. He just sat back in his big brown leather overstuffed chair, slowly closed his eyes, folded his time-worn hands together, and made a very matter-of-fact statement. "No, honey. I don't think we ever get it figured out until it's time to check out." •

My Mother's Book

Carla Bravo, Huntington Beach, California

For years my mother would tell me stories of her youth and places she had traveled. She'd always end each tale with "I should write that down," knowing full well she never would. Without telling her, I began to write her life story. I researched where she grew up, went to school, worked, and lived. I mapped out all the places she had visited and the important people she had met. I included many wonderful pictures and had it bound. When she became ill with lung cancer, I flew from California to Michigan to take care of her. In my hand was that book. There are no words to describe how happy she was or how important those pages made her feel. She showed it to everyone. When she passed away, it was on the table by her bed. My gift of love helped her leave this world in peace. •

We Love the Smell of Jet Fuel in the Morning

Isaac Cubillos, Port Saint Lucie, Florida

My sister and I grew up poor, but we didn't know it. We lived in a navy town, and our favorite weekend adventure was boarding the warships, even when the public wasn't invited. It was one place we were never turned away. We loved the smell of jet fuel in the morning. Each time, a crew member would ask, "Have you eaten?" We'd shake our heads, which always meant no, and away we went to the mess hall. Navy chow was the best, especially on an aircraft carrier. As we became adults, we realized the sailors recognized our plight and fed us attention and food. We're doing well today, and rarely get on board a Navy ship. But when we do, we inhale the diesel, machine oil mixed with jet fuel; we smile and remember those days of adventure and Navy chow. We'll always have a soft heart for sailors. •

Mother Nature's Stage

Kathryn Preston, Traverse City, Michigan

Not long after I was raped, I went into the woods. As I hiked, two deer were on the hillside above me. I lay on the ground watching them, but they didn't move. Gingerly, I moved forward. I'd only taken two steps when something rustled in the brush. It was a deer, hit by a car and dying in front of my eyes. I've never seen anything so profound. The deer glared at me with an intense mixture of wild fear and self-protection. Yet it was becoming so weak that as its eyes bore through me, its neck muscles began to weaken and the deer began to wobble in slow, concentric circles. I've never seen such a simultaneous display of strength and vulnerability. I know this event was a story enacted for me on Mother Nature's stage for clarity. The deer's death was a reflection of my inner reality. •

Sunday Car Ride

Anne Cavanaugh-Sawan, Medfield, Massachusetts

I remember a hot, crowded, wood-paneled station wagon. The windows cranked all the way down to let in a desperately needed cool breeze. No car seats or seat belts, just kids piled together. Legs jumbled upon arms, across stomachs. A lucky few in the way back, facing out, making faces at the cars behind us. Bologna sandwiches, lemonade, mixed with the smell of diesel. Mom and Dad in the front. The AM radio playing the Bruins-Canadians game. The newspaper spread across Mom's lap, her black hair tucked neatly back. A few bags of just-picked apples from the orchard safely stashed between the seats, promises of apple pie, apple cakes, applesauce. Dad pulling off suddenly to a roadside ice cream stand. "Who wants a cone? Only chocolate or vanilla, none of those fancy flavors." Bodies unwinding. Heads poking up. Doors opened, we tumbled out. That is what I remember. •

Following Directions

JoAnn Cohen, Havertown, Pennsylvania

I looked away, settling in a lounge chair, and it happened. Stephen, my four-year-old son, disappeared. He was playing in a swimming pool one moment, and then he was missing. I scanned the water more carefully. No Stephen. I asked the lifeguard, who shook her head. Only a mother could react with the intense panic that flooded me. For twenty-five minutes, I searched frantically for a boy in a red swimsuit. Then I noticed an announcement being repeated. "If you are looking for a lost child, come to the courtesy booth." I reached the booth breathless and noticed Stephen seated, leafing through a brochure. He looked up. "Mom! Where have you been?" he demanded. "Don't you remember telling me to come here if I couldn't find you? Well? Here I am!!!" I shook my head. If only I could follow directions as well as Stephen. •

My First Marathon...26.2 in 4:25

Krista Selph, Elizabethtown, Kentucky

Early morning, cold air, thirtieth birthday gift to myself, here we go. Fast pace, feeling easy, passing on the left and right; feels like how fast things have moved in the last ten years. Mile six, people turn back for the half. Twenty to go seems intimidating, like the tasks in front of me as I support a family while my husband is in Afghanistan. Mile thirteen, still having fun... slowing down but thinking about parenting and how four babies changed things but how great each second is. Mile twenty-one...this seems impossible...like running a coffee shop in a bad economy while working full time and finishing my PhD... what was I thinking? Mile twenty-six...tears as I see my best friend waiting when I thought I could finish alone...wishing it was my husband but knowing my family is why I can and will persist with this exciting, painful, priceless thing we call life. •

My Littlest Friend

Sydney Turnbull, Huntington, West Virginia

My littlest friend had long silver whiskers, black shoe button eyes, and an always-wagging tail. He was a Kleenex stealer, a carpet wetter, and the sunshine on a rainy day. He was never mad and always ready to go for a walk. He was intrigued with everything, and his eyes always asked the same question, "Did you ever see THAT before?" It made no difference to him whether we were pretty or ugly, rich or poor; he loved us unconditionally. This is God's love in action. He put man's best friend on Earth to give us a loving companion and one to look at us through eyes not blinded by worldly distractions. Part of my heart will always miss my littlest friend, but more love is there because of him. Sad though I am, I wouldn't have missed knowing him for the world! •

Legacy

Katharine Hanschu, Harrison, Arkansas

Grandpa was a man of integrity. He was a rancher who loved his family fiercely, and he passed down simple, yet important, life lessons. My dad tells a story about helping his dad tediously wash borrowed farm equipment before they returned it to a neighbor. "Why are we cleaning this?" he asked. "It was dirty when we got it." "Always return something a little better than you found it" was Grandpa's reply. A week after Grandpa's funeral, I helped my dad vacuum, wash, and refuel a car that he had borrowed from a friend. After returning the vehicle, the friend leaned over to me and remarked, "Whenever I loan something to your dad, I know it will come back in even better shape." And that is my grandpa's legacy. He left the world just a little better than he found it. I hope I can do the same. •

Out of the Blue

Julie Turner, DeFuniak Springs, Florida

As a child, I cherished a close personal relationship with God. Life went on and, as it often does, led me down a series of twisted and winding roads that ultimately led me farther away from that beloved bond. I became a mother at the tender age of nineteen, and it never occurred to me to introduce my son, AJ, to someone who had meant so much to me. One day, when AJ was four years old, he climbed into my lap as he often did. He wrapped his tiny arms around my neck and said to me out of the blue, "When I was in Heaven, before I was born, I saw you and told God I want you to be my mommy 'cause you were the beautifulest lady on Earth." Obviously, they had already met. •

A Child's American Dream

Betts Flores, Granite Bay, California

Here I am decked out for my First Communion, tap dancing… shoes and all! My tap shoes, glowing with heaps of Vaseline, are my childhood trademark. Me and my tap shoes tap to the little store for milk and candy; we tap next door to play; we tap to school, tapping in soft baby-steps in the classroom and letting it all out on the black tar playground until even my own ears complain. For Mama, a widow with seven children, the opportunity for tap dancing lessons is out of the question. Nevertheless, in my heart, my tap shoes keep me happy as a lark; visitors actually applaud my rendition of "Tea for Two." My tap shoes represent my childhood's American Dream. We may be poor migrant workers, but my tap shoes make me feel rich in so many ways. •

Blue Laundry

Teri Jones, Richfield, Ohio

Twenty-three years ago, I became a firefighter's wife. I was told that it was going to be tough, but no one told me about the blue laundry. Tons of blue laundry, saturated with the smell of smoke, sweat, and other things. It seemed an endless cycle. Year after year, he would bring home more blue shirts and blue pants, and all I could say was "No! Not more blue laundry!" Then September 11, 2001, happened. As we sat in the living room watching his firefighter brothers rushing into a flaming building, I turned to him and said, "Why would they run into that?" He turned to me and said simply, "Because that's our job." So that night as I put yet another load of blue laundry in the washing machine, I decided that maybe a little blue laundry was not such a big deal after all. •

I Choose to
Continue Living

Leslie Kimiko Ward, Anchorage, Alaska

Sometimes this choice isn't easy. Sometimes I'm incredibly homesick for the Great Collective we leave at birth and will return to again someday. Sometimes the trials of being human, the pain we express and endure, feel like too much, and I weigh my choice against its opposite. Sometimes the two come out almost even. In Alaska, where I live, lots of people choose suicide. Every year I know at least one. One year I knew three. Last year, in my friend's village of 350 people, three chose suicide. I went to the village and taught the children how to fold origami cranes to practice making something beautiful. In just a few days, we folded over 1,000 cranes. I keep a strand in my car. The rest are on display in the school library. Through this experience, I remember that I am making the right choice. •

Serenity and Hope

Dawn Wilkerson, Lake City, Florida

In 2008, at the end of a complicated pregnancy, we lost our infant son. The pain was tremendous. Then, in mid-2009, we found out I was six weeks into an even more complicated pregnancy. I tried to be hopeful, but there were so many telling me how dark the future looked. As predicted, we were rushed to the hospital—three months early. She weighed two pounds, thirteen ounces at delivery and was given only a fifty percent chance of survival. I began to give up; she began to fight. I watched her smile through pain, tubes, and surgeries. She laughed at their restrictions and limitations. At two years old, young Serenity has already taught me many lessons: Hope is always alive, you should never let others define your strengths, and living life bound by restrictions and limitations can only keep you from being the person you are capable of becoming. •

The Last Piece of the Puzzle

Amy Gravino, Port Jefferson, New York

Imagine your daughter. What does she look like? Maybe she is small. Maybe she wears glasses. Does she have friends? Maybe she is the girl huddled in the corner at birthday parties, crying from being chased around with balloons by the other children, who know the noise of the balloons popping frightens her. Maybe she comes home from school, nine years old, nine long years, and tells you she feels like killing herself. Maybe she sits in the guidance counselor's office the next afternoon, trying to hold everything in her together for just one more day. Maybe she grows up, a girl on the autism spectrum who now is a young woman, finding her way in a world that said there was no place for her. Maybe she is helping others with autism spectrum disorders who face the same path that she herself once traveled. Maybe she is me. •

A Few Words about My Wife

James McDonaugh , Irmo, South Carolina

Running a marathon is hard. Running one blind with no assistance is unthinkable unless you're my wife, Amy. At eleven, surgeries on a vascular anomaly in her face left Amy blind in her right eye with 20/400 vision in her left and no peripheral. Doctors advised against pregnancy and sports. In 2004, following the birth of our third child, Amy began running as a way to get back in shape and enjoy a short break from her responsibilities at home. She steadily improved in speed and stamina and began competing in 5-K races. Amy ran her first marathon in 2009 and qualified for Boston, which she ran the following year. On May 1, 2011, Amy won the Flying Pig Marathon in Cincinnati in 2:58:10, just weeks after emergency surgery on her right cheek. Amy's health issues persist, but so does her refusal to be confined or defined by her condition. •

From Broken Home to Mended Fence

Jeannie O'Sullivan, Audubon, New Jersey

I was eight when my parents sat me down and gently told me they were divorcing, a moment that shattered my sense of well-being and sealed my conviction that a successful union wasn't possible. Over the next three decades, my father remarried and separated again, my siblings and I navigated our own romances, and my parents gradually mended fences as family tragedies and triumphs, including my mother's severe respiratory disease, forced their interaction. My father visited my mother daily during the last months of her life and was at her bedside when she took her final breath in May. The lesson learned—that relationships evolve, change, and don't necessarily follow convention—was perfectly encapsulated in how my mother had filled out her hospital paperwork. She listed my dad as the emergency contact and, in the How Known field, wrote "Friend." •

The Sunny Side of Food Phobias

David Kuhn, Newington, Connecticut

I loved eggs as a toddler. I consumed them in such copious quantities that my parents might have shrewdly invested in a coop and a few score hens just to keep me sated. My gluttonous affair with eggs continued until the day my rock star big sister proclaimed them "yucky." That was more than thirty-five egg-less years ago. But there it was, the second course in a tasting menu my fiancé had treated us to: ravioli un uovo in sage brown butter. Tucked inside this pasta parcel was perched a perfectly runny bit of yolk atop a nest of herbed ricotta. I steeled myself against its undoubted awfulness and put food and fork to mouth. From the first bite, I was ensorcelled. Eating this thing was like consuming a bit of ambrosia: I felt nearly immortal while I savored its rich, golden goodness. Can anyone spare a coop? •

Sons and War

Dawn Endrijaitis, Independence, Missouri

How do you send your son to war? It goes against everything you've spent a lifetime preventing. You might as well let him run with scissors or ride in the car without a seat belt. All those nights you lay awake waiting for him to make curfew don't come close to watching him board that plan to Afghanistan. As you hug him one last time, you wonder why it was so important to make him sit up straight and take smaller bites. He's going to war. There will be no one to make sure he eats his vegetables or wears clean socks. How do you send your son to war? You give him a hug and kiss him gently on the cheek and then fall to your knees and pray that God will let you experience his return. •

All These Things
Plus One

Nicole Malato, Toms River, New Jersey

I am a wife, a mother, a daughter, and a sister. I am an aunt, a niece, a cousin, and a friend. I'm an HR manager and a Mary Kay consultant. I'm an experienced bridesmaid. I was the head of my church youth group. I'm an MBA graduate. I am not a great dancer; I'm a klutz. I'm one who helps others, and I'm a Roman Catholic. I'm a country music fan and a BlackBerry junkie. I am blessed with amazing family and friends. I am strong. I am an allergy-sufferer. I am one who loves to laugh. I am afraid of heights. I'm a Jersey girl, with an honorary Pennsylvania girl membership. I'm a fan of the smell of sunblock, cigars, and roses. I am a scatterbrain. And I am one more thing. I am a breast cancer patient. And someday I will be a breast cancer survivor. •

My Wedding Day

Darleene Hancock, Riverside, California

Fifty-four years ago, my husband and I eloped to Yuma, Arizona. Through a comedy of errors, bad directions, changes in law, and a gap in justices being sworn in, we were finally married in a little casino connected to a tiny dinner in Searchlight, Nevada. For wedding rings, all we had was a party favor fake ring I found in the bottom of my purse. The justice of the peace shook his head, gave Fred a sad look, and married us anyway. We could pay him only two dollars because that was all we had left in our pockets. Luckily, the gas station attendant gave us a wedding present of a full tank of gas. Our life together followed suit: full of comedy, errors, and many directions but nevertheless very happy, with eight children and, so far, seven grandchildren. And I wouldn't trade that wedding day for anything. •

September 10

Janie Zabala Mayer, Antelope, California

I met him that morning in Central Park. He had been away at school for what had seemed like an eternity. There was no agenda. We picnicked. We talked about the future. We played a game in which we kissed while sitting on every bench that we encountered. He held my hand and said my face was more radiant than the sunshine upon us and my lips were softer than the cool afternoon breeze. He would start his new job in Lower Manhattan the following day, but he set that day aside for me. I will always remember that beautiful day, September 10, 2001. •

This Rings True...

Grant Hester, Los Angeles, California

Andrew was six when he asked to borrow five dollars. He returned with a ring and proudly handed it to me. "Dad, I bought it for you." He beamed, as did I. Ten years passed and the ring remained on my finger. I was walking my dog when I happened upon two men who accosted me. During that incident, the ring was lost. I searched frantically for it, but it was never found. Returning from work one afternoon, a red bag hung from my doorknob. Inside was a bulky gold watch. No one admitted to leaving it for me. I decided to have it sized. The jeweler took the watch in the back while I browsed through his many cases. One piece caught my eye. It was the very ring my son had given me. It fit the impression on my finger perfectly. I suppose time does heal all wounds. •

Cancer, Faith, and a Pastrami Sandwich

Larissa Allen, Visalia, California

Sitting in a hospital bed with chemo chasing after late-stage colon cancer, I was at an emotional low when a gentleman pushed back my curtain and offered to make me a pastrami sandwich. I protested, but he said he had been at his wife's side when she went through cancer and knew this was a way to give back. "To eat is to heal" were his words as he smiled and backed out of the room. My husband pushed the plate toward me, and I took a bite, soon inhaling the entire sandwich. I will never know why my stomach accepted that sandwich or why it didn't taste like tin. I just ate it like I had never eaten before. Someone else who had walked in my shoes so boldly saying, "To eat is to heal," made me think about how far a little faith can take you. •

The Man with
the Tattoos

Chance Steeves, Riverview, New Brunswick, Canada

My father had all sorts of interesting friends. I remember one in particular: He was tall and large and had more hair than he knew what to do with. His arms were covered in ink, a tangle of reds and blues and black that reminded me of chalk drawings on a faded driveway. He came to our house and spoke with my father about the adult things grown folk talk about. I paraded into the living room with my stuffed animals and Disney dolls and explained to him everything he needed to know about the things that were important to a five-year-old like me. He listened and smiled and held all the toys I pushed into his arms. Before he left, he stopped at the stairs and turned to me. He smiled and thanked me. Why? "You're the only child I've met who isn't afraid of me." •

I Hated My Parents

Fran Samuelson, Liberty Hill, Texas

I hated my parents. I hated them with all the bile that could be generated by a seven-year-old. I convinced my little brother to hate them, too. To exact revenge, we would run away. We ate breakfast, made peanut butter sandwiches, and took cookies, summer sausage, and thermoses of juice. We went first to the creek and watched the minnows swim for our lunch crumbs. Then we went to the dairy farm, helped the farmer pen his calves, stall and milk his cows, feed his cows. We sat in the shade under the dilapidated buckboard, examined our empty thermoses, and decided that we were cruel. We went home expecting police cars and tears. Our parents were still in bed. •

Nothing Is Ever Free

Robin Lee, Jamestown, South Carolina

When I was six and my brother was five, our mom allowed us to walk to the corner store to buy some candy. As we approached the front of the store, I witnessed a man taking Coke bottles out of the outdoor refrigerated case, and he put them in his car and drove away. I looked at my brother and said, "Cokes are free today!" We loaded up as many as we could carry and headed for home. When I told Mom about the free Cokes, she marched us back to the store and made us return the drinks and tell the clerk we were sorry. Mom explained that the customer had paid for the drinks first inside the store and then came outside to get his purchases and leave. And then she said those words that have been seared into my brain ever since: "Nothing is ever free." •

It All Counts

Donna Jarvis, Hollis Center, Maine

At age twenty-three, a rhinoceros charged me. I bungee jumped into a canyon. And I dodged bullets in a crossfire in Kashmir. At forty-three, I have a day job and mortgage. I do laundry and dishes. I drive a sensible family vehicle and hang out at Little League fields. I don't believe my story is unique. Only the details separate me from any middle-aged woman who must learn to navigate the daily mundane with the identity of her free-spirited youth. My former "life" is no more extraordinary than the beauty and grace revealed in the ordinary…a kayak ride in the early morning mist…a harvest moon…watching my children breathe as they sleep. If life is a journey and not a destination, then each stage holds the possibility for magic. And somewhere between star-gazing in my twenties and grocery shopping in my forties, I have to believe…it all counts. •

Surf Soldiers

Caroline McCandless, San Diego, California

We're just kids, twenty-somethings sitting around a beach bonfire, drinking beer, and telling stories. It's been a long day, but our faces glow with more than firelight. Daniel and I love traveling, and we talk about where he traveled before Afghanistan. They all cringe as they recall the smell of the poop lakes in Iraq, and Dorian laughs loudly. We're just kids at the beach, but I realize what an outsider must see. I'm surrounded by young soldiers, young vets, single/double amputees in wheelchairs, burn victims relaxing in the shadows, glass eyes twinkling from the flames. They're wounded soldiers I'm helping rehabilitate with "surf therapy." We surfed all day today and we'll surf all day tomorrow. That's what an outsider would see, but in my mind, I'm just a girl with a surfboard sitting among heroes, trying to make them feel like a couple of kids at the beach. •

Story Time

Heather Farnath, Cherry Hill, New Jersey

Weekends at my house are a blur of errands, muddy cleats, and half-finished home improvement projects. The whole family is over, the windows are open, the game is on, the house smells like fall and dinner and bleach. It takes approximately one afternoon for my kids to put their toys back exactly where they belong: the living room floor. "This place was clean this morning," I say. "Don't worry about it," Mom says. "This is such a precious time in life. Be careful you don't miss it." She smiles when my son spills his drink, laughs as she pulls corn out of my hair. By the time everyone leaves, I'm exhausted. I forget the dishes in the sink and rest my head on my husband's chest. "Look," he says as my daughter climbs up onto her brother's lap for a story. I listen, thankful I didn't miss it. •

Primatology

J. J. Keith, Los Angeles, California

"No. Not ape. That's monkey." She's two-and-a-half, and the one thing she knows for sure is that the rhesus monkey at the zoo is an ape. Maybe she'd get away misidentifying primates if she had a different mom. I whisper, "I have a degree in physical anthropology and I'm telling you that's a monkey. He has a tail. Apes don't have tails." I look around, relieved that no one heard me debating with a toddler. She pats me on the shoulder and condescends beyond her years. "No, Mom. That's a monkey." I've met my match, or rather I made her. I'm on the other side of myself now. I spent the first thirty years of my life correcting people, and now I'll spend the next thirty being corrected. I deserve it, but my poor husband. He didn't ask for two of me. •

Highway Sixty-Four

Ailene Everts, Williams, Arizona

I work at a gas station on a busy highway on the way to a popular tourist site. It's not a glamorous job—I clean bathrooms, I pick up trash, I mop floors, and I handle your oft-circulated cash. I muddle through the language barriers, the difference in cultures, and sometimes it takes a game of charades to get the point across. There are days when your patience wears thin with me just as mine does with you. And Lord knows, I don't make a lot of money. But through this job, through the heavy accents of your foreign tongue and the long hours I work every day, I have learned lessons that could have never been taught in school through books or lectures—patience, understanding, tolerance, and acceptance. Acceptance that you are you, I am me, and that while we're all different, we're all still, a "we." •

The Beauty Blade

Elisabeth McKetta, Boise, Idaho

Midday, on a Snake River camping trip, a rabid bat attacked my husband. I was pregnant, new to Idaho, and didn't trust the wilderness with my big belly and animal hunger. He got shots. We waited. And I wondered: Where does this happen? In other places I've lived, nobody worries about rabies. If he dies, would I stay in Idaho? Could I raise my daughter in this dry-grassed place where risk comes from nature and not people, where poison hemlock grows wild and foxes pounce upon hand-fed songbirds, where the blade between death and new life stays forever sharp? That blade is where beauty lies, where stories emerge. Before I knew he would live, I already knew I would stay. •

A Bonding Moment

Rebecca Jamison, Emporia, Kansas

I sat in a rocking chair, holding my sleeping three-week-old son. He wasn't sleeping through the night. He was always fussy and only slept two hours at a time. I felt like I was a failure. I was sure I was doing everything wrong. Overcome with emotions, I began to cry. I looked down at my son and was surprised to see he was awake and staring at me intently. I looked down and met his gaze. We sat there for a moment gazing at each other and then simultaneously we both grinned. The wonder of the moment caused me to laugh out loud. At the sound of my laugh, his grin widened into a full open-mouth smile. At that moment, I let my anxieties go and began to focus solely on the joys of being a mother. •

My Butterfly

Patricia Anderson, Webster, Wisconsin

I noticed her sitting alone and sobbing. I asked her, "What's the matter, honey?" She told me she "didn't want to live here anymore." I asked, "Where do you want to live?" She said, "I want to live where there is a ball and a swing." I said, "We have a ball and swing." With tears, she replied, "But there are no kids." Kids like herself. She didn't know group homes existed, only the hospital unit she'd experienced with special needs kids. Our girl is challenged with autism. At fourteen, she knew living with kids like herself would mean having to sacrifice living with her own family. And she did. We knew she had to go. "I like living here." She tells me on the telephone, "I love you." I tell her through the lump in my throat, "I love you, too, honey. I'm so proud of you." •

A Real Love Story—
Fairy Tales Do Happen

Elliot Levanthal, Tustin, California

In 1985 at twenty-five years old, I briefly crossed paths in New Zealand with a beautiful Australian nurse named Julie. My next stop was Melbourne, Australia. I spent three days with Julie before a flight to Brisbane, Australia. Realizing my mistake of leaving the love of my life, I took a twenty-four-hour bus ride back to her. After seven more romantic days, never leaving each other's side, sadly I had to return to America for work. We corresponded by mail for months (before Internet), and I gave her a Minnie Mouse for a gift. We lost contact and moved on with our lives due to distance and marriages, and subsequently failed marriages. Twenty-five years later, reuniting on Facebook, our romance blossomed. She had kept the Minnie Mouse. In July 2011, I proposed to my princess at the Disneyland Castle and on October 1, 2011, we got married in Las Vegas. •

Making Friends with My Kitchen

Dana Hinders, Clarksville, Iowa

When my son's kindergarten teacher had the kids draw pictures of their moms, he drew me baking a birthday cake. A note on my refrigerator says, "Deer Mom. Yor fud is gud." (Translation: Dear Mom. Your food is good.) If you asked me what I did best, cooking would be far down on the list. I cook out of necessity. Hungry family + tight budget = being forced to become friends with my kitchen. I didn't have cash for a bakery birthday cake, and the meal that inspired my son's note was made out of leftovers and random cans from my pantry. One day, after getting frustrated by a recipe that wouldn't turn out, I asked my son why he thought I was a good cook. "Because you love us," he said, as he reached over to give me a kiss on the cheek. Yup. That works for me. •

Katrina and Magnolias

Cathy Suarez, Hattiesburg, Mississippi

It was the only place I could look without sobbing: the sky. For the entire world that my eyes could see, there was nothing but wreckage from the savage storm. Giant trees ripped from their roots deep within the earth and tossed around like toy cars in a child's tantrum. Our home so lovingly built now bore the weight of the magnificent old trees, crushing the roof under mighty limbs. "God, where can I look and not see total chaos?" I looked up through tears when the answer whispered on the wind of a crystal clear blue sky. "Yes, Lord, the sky is clean!" It was the start of a new life, there in the midst of pain. For all her might, Katrina had not won! New life and hope really can blossom and spring forth in abundance if only we are willing to see through eyes of gratitude! •

Microwave Toast

Barbara Gode Wiles, Cheshire, Connecticut

The fire in the microwave is out and the microwave is fried, but I guess that doesn't really matter without a little background. Alan is fifty-five and my husband of twenty-five years, and I am losing him to a world I can't see or imagine. The Parkinson's diagnosis I could live with, but the dementia is frightening. He wanted toast, so he put the bread in the microwave and set it for five minutes. I live in a house filled with smoke, dragons, purple dogs, people partying all the time, six-inch grizzly bears, and every other thing you can imagine. None of it frightens him...it is just all there all the time for him. He knows who I am but isn't always sure how to shower or dress. I am losing him to a world that will take him away from me forever, but he'll still be here. •

Stitches in Time

Maureen Haggerty, Chalfont, Pennsylvania

Brian's photograph captured his grandmother as I remembered her. Marie loved to knit, creating a rainbow of tiny sweaters for new or expectant mothers among her only granddaughter's circle of friends. After Marie's death, my cousin Jeanne came across the last sweater her mother had made and realized it was the perfect gift for her own daughter's baby shower. Knowing there would be tears, Jeanne decided to present her gift after the others had been opened. What she didn't know was that each of the guests, without discussing it with the others, had decided to give Patricia the sweater Marie had made for her baby. Some of the sweaters were a bit frayed or faded from frequent wearing and washing. Tiny fingers had tugged some slightly out of shape. But every stitch was infused with generations of love that now warms Patricia's sons: Liam, Owen, and Jack. •

For Adrian, 150 Blessings Disguised as Words

Eleni Zaharopoulos, Brooklyn, New York

I was born to Greeks, socialized in Queens, suffered school, raised wrong, then right, then wrong again. I felt love—six years strong. I've gone mad. I've touched God's hands. I've stretched this heart from east to west. I've seen my father in his final rest. I've made love upon the water's edge. I've met the man I was to wed. We shared quite a life, but then he died. My feet have traveled far and wide, my eyes have cried a million tears, my head has held a weary spine, my heart's been known to praise the sky, and I've been told I like to rhyme. I was born in May, on its eighth day. My Jesus year is upon my heels, I'm barely past my troubled years. My life has held momentous things. Sometimes I think it's best to sing, and laugh and dance dance dance dance dance. •

Documenting My Life

Joshua Hawker, Spokane Valley, Washington

I make journals, but that's not what this story is about. It's more about what I fill these journals up with, more about the need I feel to document every aspect of my existence. Why do I feel so compelled to record my life? I understand recording special moments like when I got married or when we had our three children. But why do I feel the need to record myself making coleslaw, brushing my teeth, or even sleeping? Maybe I record because it's fun to remember the past, maybe I record to catch glimpses of who I really am. Maybe I record so that my children can see just how silly their papa was. Maybe it's all of these. Perhaps recording is my way of authoring the story of my life. With each new page in my journal or each new tape, it's a new beginning. •

You Come and You Go

Cathy Cook, Corona, California

My son recently died at age thirty-six—young by the world's standards. Disabilities left him as a five-year-old, completely uninhibited. He "fired" people long before Donald Trump! He loved to pull out his imaginary gun (thumb and forefinger) and shout, "Bang!" when he didn't like something someone said. Then, he'd crack a smile and let out a big belly laugh. A while ago someone famous died, and Aaron said convincingly, "Mom, you know what? You come and you go." He was right! That's about as simple as you can get when describing life on Earth—you come and you go. Over a hundred people attended his service, many giving glowing accounts of his zest for life and how he made them laugh. The lesson Aaron taught is that life is short, and what better way to leave than to leave as a friend, and a funny friend at that. •

The Summer Nights of My Youth

Becky Mantooth, Arlington, Texas

I remember the summer nights of my youth. A time filled with catching fireflies by the jarful, playing games of chase and hide and seek by the light of the moon, or lying on the ground searching for the constellations in the sky. The family would gather on our porch, sipping hot coffee or sweet iced tea. Our entertainment would be the telling and listening of stories or the blending of our voices as we sang in sweet harmony. When the night would call us to our beds, I would face the open window, gazing up at the stars in the sky. The gentle wind would fragrance my bedroom with the aroma of the honeysuckle that grew outside. The sounds of nature and the train's whistle would lullaby me into the land of my dreams, as a shooting star would bid me good night. •

The Man with Cancer

Liz Deardorff, Cincinnati, Ohio

I overheard a conversation once: "You ever sell that condo? You know, the one that belonged to the man with cancer?" I wondered, "What is the man with cancer's name? What story does he have?" I wondered, "When people talk about my dad, do they call him 'the man with cancer?'" He has a name. He has a story. We are all people with names and stories. We say we know this, yet somehow we are still labeled. Left me to wonder, "What do people see when they look at me?" •

This Thing…

Jodi Peppard-Latocki, Ypsilanti, Michigan

It's something we take for granted every day. It flies by without notice. It's full of incredible adventures, risks, and chances. It's filled with memories. It has its ups and downs. It brings tears and laughter. Each chapter brings new stories and with it new insight. Through it, we grow in wisdom and learn from mistakes. From it, we make choices. Everyone has their own with their very own personal story. Some end quickly, while others make history. We can gripe about it all too often and not appreciate it until it is about over. There is nothing like it and never will be. It's precious. This thing called life. •

Write your own entry! In 150 words or less, share a lesson, simple advice, funny moment or other story from your life.

Write your own entry! In 150 words or less, share a lesson, simple advice, funny moment or other story from your life.

....

....

....

....

....

....

....

....

Write your own entry! In 150 words or less, share a lesson, simple advice, funny moment or other story from your life.

Write your own entry! In 150 words or less, share a lesson, simple advice, funny moment or other story from your life.

....

....

....

....

....

....

....

....

....

Write your own entry! In 150 words or less, share a lesson, simple advice, funny moment or other story from your life.

....

....

....

....

....

....

....

....

....

Index of Contributors

Note: The twelve contributors labeled as winners had their entries published in the March 2012 edition of *Reader's Digest* magazine.

Aiello, William	64	Endrijaitis, Dawn ... 133
Allen, Larissa	139	Everts, Ailene ... 148
Anderson, Patricia	151	Falk, Brian ... 91
Arbide, Alejandro	2	Farnath, Heather ... 145
Archibald, Diane	3	Flores, Betts ... 125
Baez, Hethyre	26	Gaal, Steve ... 13
Baum, Karen	62	Gaertner, Gary ... 75
Bias, Ashley	67	Gerding, Linda ... 53
Blowers, Mary DeKok	108	Gifford, Alicia ... 25
Boyce, Julia (Winner)	**110**	Goethals, Kristin ... 100
Bravo, Carla	115	Goldstein, Betty ... 14
Brown, Deanne	95	Gostley, Lula Mae ... 74
Campion, Daniel	11	Grantham, Greg ... 46
Cardinal, Ann	40	Gravino, Amy ... 129
Cavanaugh-Sawan, Anne	118	Green, Shereen Hart ... 114
Chadwick, Loretta	29	Gross, Amy ... 28
Chandra, Leah	16	Guillot, Laura ... 104
Christians, Tamara	80	**Hagar, Audrey (Winner)** ... **20**
Christoforakis, Jenny	27	Haggerty, Maureen ... 156
Cisneros, Deanna	58	Hamilton, C.A. ... 30
Cline, Misty	78	Hancock, Darleene ... 136
Cohen, Ashley	86	**Hanschu, Katharine (Winner)** ... **122**
Cohen, JoAnn	119	Harris, Aimee ... 60
Cook, Cathy	159	Harris, Brandy ... 63
Counts, Charlotte	68	Harris, Kimberly ... 18
Cubillos, Isaac	116	Hartman, Tamira ... 19
Dahl, Karen (Winner)	**38**	Hawker, Joshua ... 158
de Lagarde, Julie	106	Hester, Grant ... 138
Deardorff, Liz	161	Hinders, Dana ... 153
Dedeo, Michelle	69	Hoerner, Keith ... 81
Detamore, Guida	7	Holland, Jannie ... 41
Dillman, Lara	79	Hunter, Lindsay ... 31
Dornich, Joe	42	Jamison, Rebecca ... 150
Duwaik, Anissa	50	Jandereski, Kaitlin ... 90
Dykema, Jennifer	43	Jarden, Dennis ... 103

Jarvis, Donna. 143
Jennings, James 15
Johnson, Katherine Doe. 94
Jones, Leslie 36
Jones, Teri. 126
Kearney, William 47
Keith, J.J. (Winner). 146
Kelly, Casie. 109
Kennedy, Vickey Malone. 6
Kilen, Josh. 101
Kingsley, Katherine 83
Kleinfield-Hayes, Marni. 35
Kuhn, David. 132
Lee, Robin 142
Levanthal, Elliot. 152
Malato, Nicole (Winner) 135
Mantooth, Becky. 160
Marino, Lauren 23
May, Bruce. 12
Mayer, Brian (Winner). 32
Mayer, Janie Zabala. 137
Mazioum, Iman 98
McAllister, Andrea. 77
McCandless, Caroline. 144
McCarthy, Kevin 66
McDonaugh, James 130
McGowan, Angela. 44
McKetta, Elisabeth 149
McNamara, Nan 10
Mendivel, Sarah. 65
Montana, Heather. 88
Moore, Jim 49
Morris, Brian 37
Nollman, Barbara 22
O'Sullivan, Jeannie 131
Paden, Ann 57
Pantuliano, Livia 48
Pasto, Robyn 51
Paton, Judy 24
Pengal, Chelsee. 92
Peppard-Latocki, Jodi. 162

Preston, Kathryn. 117
Revilla, Gabriela. 56
Rhatigan, Joe. 34
Rickert, Dorothy 82
Riley, Keri. 61
Ritter, Lynda 76
Roach, Chely (Winner) 70
Roberto, Michael. 87
Rohloff, Greg. 105
Roth, Courtney
  (Readers' Choice Winner) 84
Rowe, Deborah 59
Ruland, Jim (Grand-Prize Winner) . . .8
Samuelson, Fran 141
Schaller, Amy. 17
Selph, Krista. 120
Shearer, Jayne. 73
Spencer, Davalynn. 5
Steeves, Chance 140
Stimpson, Jennifer 33
Suarez, Cathy. 154
Sulfridge, Katy. 113
Sumsion, Linda 107
Teeter, Deborah 89
Thomas, Arthur. 72
Thompson, Meghan (Winner) 54
Traywick, Flo 4
Turnbull, Sydney 121
Turner, Julie. 124
Vajraca, Sabina 99
Vakanas, Carole. 52
Vickery, Kit. 45
Ward, Leslie Kimiko. 127
Weisman, Michele. 102
Wiles, Barbara Gode 155
Wilkerson, Dawn. 128
Zaharopoulos, Eleni 157
Zane, Valerie 93
Zeidler, Erik (Winner) 96
Zindler, Shirley. 112

PROJECT STAFF

Executive Editor: Barbara O'Dair

Senior Editor: Andrea Au Levitt

Editors: Perri O. Blumberg, Caitlin O'Connell, Dawn Raffel, Natalie van der Meer

Editorial Assistant: Elizabeth Kelly

Copyeditor: Hope Clarke

Managing Editor: Lorraine Burton

Senior Art Director: George McKeon

Designer: Jennifer Tokarski